Excel 5

by Shelley O'Hara

alpha
books

A Division of Macmillan Computer Publishing
201 W. 103rd Street, Indianapolis, Indiana 46290 USA

Dedication

To my best friends from CHS '80—Pam, Barb, Kelley, Kathleen, and Ann.

International Standard Book Number: 1-56761-473-6

Library of Congress Catalog Card Number: 94-70073

96 95 94   8 7 6 5 4 3 2 1

Interpretation of the printing code: the rightmost number of the first series of numbers is the year of the book's printing; the rightmost number of the second series of numbers is the number of the book's printing. For example, a printing code of 94-1 shows that the first printing of the book occurred in 1994.

Printed in the United States of America

Publisher   *Marie Butler-Knight*

Managing Editor   *Elizabeth Keaffaber*

Acquisitions Manager   *Barry Pruett*

Product Development Manager   *Faithe Wempen*

Development Editor   *Kelly Oliver*

Production Editor   *Michelle Shaw*

Copy Editor   *Audra Gable*

Cover Designer   *Tim Amrhein*

Designer   *Barbara Webster*

Indexer   *Bront Davis*

Production Team   *Gary Adair, Dan Caparo, Brad Chinn, Kim Cofer, Mark Enochs, Stephanie Gregory, Jenny Kucera, Beth Rago, Bobbi Satterfield, Marc Shecter, Greg Simsic, Kris Simmons, Carol Stamile, Robert Wolf*

Special thanks to C. Herbert Feltner for ensuring the technical accuracy of this book.

Introduction

Using a program like Excel 5 is supposed to make working with numbers easy, but many new users find the program *difficult*. The manual and most instructional books cover each and every feature in pages upon pages of detail. Finding what's important and finding what you need is a frustrating process. What you need is a book that tells you only the important things. You need a cheat sheet. You need this book.

What Makes This Book Different

This book is designed to fulfill the promise of Excel 5: to make creating a spreadsheet document easy. This book weeds out extraneous information and focuses on the skills you need to create an accurate, professional spreadsheet. The following list summarizes the key features of the book:

- *Excel 5 Cheat Sheet* doesn't cover each and every feature; it covers the features you are most likely to use and will get the most benefit from. You can count on this book as a reference to the most commonly used features.

- This book is divided into about 50 chapters, each of which deals with a particular task or feature. Finding the information is easy.

- Each chapter starts with a quick cheat sheet of the most common tasks.

- Within each chapter, the most basic tasks are covered first. They are grouped into a section entitled "Basic Survival." When you are learning the program, you can focus on these tasks. When you are using the book as a reference, you can find the basic information fast.

- As you use the program more and more, you will want to learn how to fine-tune or use some of the other available options. These topics are covered after the basics section, in a section called "Beyond Survival." You can investigate these topics when you want to learn a little more about a feature or when you want to tweak how a feature works.

- Every procedure is broken down into step-by-step information and is illustrated with figures. We've made following the steps and getting the results you want as simple as possible.

- The key concepts and commands are highlighted for you—helping you quickly identify the most important information in the text.

- Common tasks, toolbar buttons, and reference information are provided on three tear-out sheets. You can use these cheat sheets as a quick reminder.

- Tips appear in the margin to draw your attention to important points and to show you shortcuts.

If you want a handy reference that's easy to use and contains all the information you need, this is the book for you.

How This Book Is Organized

This book is organized into five parts. Part 1, "Excel Basics," covers how to start and learn your way around the program. You will learn how to get help, select commands, and exit the program in this part.

Part 2, "Creating a Worksheet," covers the topics and tasks that are used to create a worksheet. You will learn how to enter different types of data, and shortcuts for entering data. You will also find out how to edit and delete data and save and open files.

Part 3, "Formatting and Printing a Worksheet," explains how to transform your document from a column of rows and numbers into a professional-looking document. You will learn how to change the font, make alignment changes, set up the page, and then finally how to print.

Part 4, "Timesavers," focuses on the timesaving features included with Excel. You will learn how to quickly find data, assign names so that formulas are easier to create and understand, check spelling, and more.

Part 5, "Excel's Special Features," covers charts and databases. You can use your worksheet data to set up a chart right on the worksheet or on another sheet. You can also use Excel as a simple database manager. This section focuses on these topics.

No matter what type of spreadsheet you create, you will find the information you need in this book.

Acknowledgments

A book is more than the work of one person. It is a collective effort by many individuals, each providing his or her own personal touch to the project and each improving the book in some way. I would like to thank the following for his or her role in this book:

Marie Butler-Knight, Publisher, for always striving to create a product that meets the needs of the computer user and book buyer.

Barry Pruett, Acquisitions Manager. Without Barry's original concept of this book, there wouldn't be a book. He dreamt up the title, concept, and key design features, and he kept the book on track from inception to final product.

Kelly Oliver, Development Editor, for her insightful suggestions, comments, and additions that improved the clarity and usefulness of the book.

Michelle Shaw, Production Editor, for managing all the pieces and parts that have to fit together to make a book.

Audra Gable, Copy Editor, for her careful editing of the text.

Herb Feltner, Technical Editor, for his technical review of the book.

Contents

Part I: Excel Basics

Part 2: Creating a Worksheet

Part 3: Formatting and Printing a Worksheet

Part 4: Timesavers

Part 5: Excel's Special Features

Excel Basics

The first step in using any program is getting familiar with the basic operation of the program: how to start, look around, get help, and exit. This section covers these basic skills, as it deals with the following topics:

- Starting Excel
- Understanding the Screen Display
- Working with Windows
- Selecting Menu Commands
- Using the Toolbars
- Getting Help
- Exiting Excel

Cheat Sheet

Starting Windows

1. At the DOS prompt, type WIN.
2. Press Enter.

Starting Excel

1. Double-click the Microsoft Office program group icon.
2. Double-click the Excel program icon.

Setting Up Windows to Start Excel Automatically

1. Double-click the Microsoft Office program group icon.
2. Double-click the Startup group icon.
3. Arrange the windows so you can see part of each window.
4. Hold down Ctrl and drag the Excel program icon to the Startup group window.

Using File Manager to Start Excel and Open a Document

1. Double-click the Main program group icon.
2. Double-click the File Manager icon.
3. Double-click the directory that contains the Excel file you want to open.
4. Double-click the file.

Starting Excel

The Program Manager, the key part of Microsoft Windows, is what you see when you start Windows. The Program Manager does just what its name implies: it manages programs and makes it easy to start any Windows program.

Basic Survival

Starting Windows

Many new computers today come with Windows installed and set up to start automatically each time you turn on the computer. You flip the power switch, and the computer starts up, performs some commands, and gives the command to start Windows. After Windows is up and running, you see the Program Manager on-screen. From the Program Manager, you can start any Windows program you want.

Remember!

On other computers, you see the DOS prompt (C:\>) when you turn on the computer. Before you can use a Windows program, you have to start Windows. To do so, **type WIN and press Enter**. When you see the Program Manager on-screen, you are ready to start Excel.

Starting Excel

Starting a program is a two-step process. First, you open the *program group* that contains the program icon. Then you double-click on the *program icon*.

Follow these steps:

1. Double-click the Microsoft Office program group icon to open the program group.

2. Double-click on the Excel program icon.

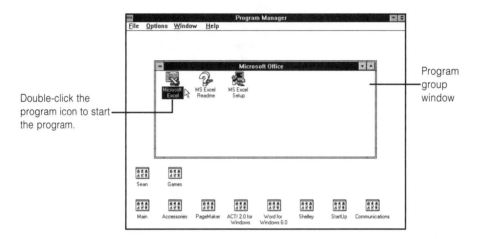

Double-click the
program icon to start
the program.

Program
group
window

A blank worksheet appears on-screen. For more information on the different parts of the Excel screen, see Chapter 2, "Understanding the Screen Display."

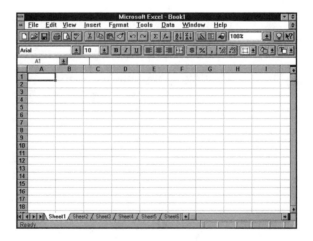

Beyond Survival

Starting Excel Automatically

If you use Excel all of the time or most of the time, you may want to set up your system so Excel starts each time you start Windows. This saves you from having to go through the process of starting Windows and then starting the program.

To start Excel automatically, you place a copy of the program icon in the Startup program group. The Startup group is a special program group created automatically by Windows. Each time you start Windows, it starts all the programs that are in the Startup group.

PuT a copy— noT The original—in The STarTup group!

To put a copy of the Excel icon in the Startup group, follow these steps:

1. Double-click the Microsoft Office program group icon. You should see the Excel program icon in the window.

2. Double-click on the Startup group icon. Now you have two windows open: the Startup window and the Microsoft Office window. (Note that your Startup group may be empty or may contain program icons other than the ones shown.)

3. Arrange the windows so that you can see at least part of each window on-screen. You can resize the windows by dragging a border. To move a window, drag the title bar. See Chapter 3, "Working with Windows," for help on moving and resizing windows.

4. Hold down the Ctrl key and drag the Microsoft Excel program icon to the Startup group window. Holding down the Ctrl key tells Windows to make a copy of the icon. To *drag*, point to the icon, press and hold the mouse button, and move the mouse. The icon moves across the screen. When the icon is in the right spot, release the mouse button and the Ctrl key.

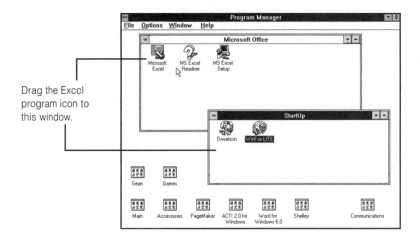

Drag the Excel
program icon to
this window.

The next time you start Windows, Excel will start automatically. If you change your mind and decide you no longer want to start Excel each time you start Windows, delete the program icon from the Startup group. To do that, click once on the icon, and then press the Delete key. When a dialog box appears, click on the Yes button to confirm the deletion.

Using File Manager to Start Excel and Open a Document

The File Manager is a program included with Windows. You use this program to work with files: to copy files, delete files, move files, and so on. For complete information on the File Manager, see your Windows manual.

In the File Manager screen, directories are listed on the left side of the window and are indicated with folder icons. The highlighted directory is the *current* or *active* directory. The right side of the window lists the files and directories in the current directory. Files are indicated with document icons. Excel files use the .XLS extension.

One of the things you can do from the File Manager is start a program and open a document at the same time. To do so, follow these steps:

1. Double-click on the Main program group icon. (The File Manager is stored in the Main program group.) You should see the File Manager icon and other program icons.

2. Double-click on the File Manager icon. It looks like a small filing cabinet. The File Manager appears on-screen.

3. Double-click on the directory that contains the file you want to open (probably the EXCEL directory).

Excel files

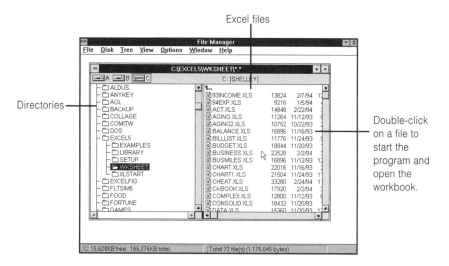

Directories

Double-click on a file to start the program and open the workbook.

4. Double-click on the Excel file you want to open. Windows starts Excel and opens the workbook. When you exit Excel, you are returned to the File Manager.

Cheat Sheet

Understanding Window Controls

- **Title bar** Displays the name of the window.
- **Control-menu box** Provides access to Control menu.
- **Maximize, Minimize, and Restore buttons** Change the window's size.

Understanding the Program Window Elements

- **Menu bar** Lists menu names.
- **Toolbar** Displays buttons that represent commands.
- **Formula bar** Displays contents of the active cell.
- **Scroll bars** Used to move to a different part of the window.
- **Status bar** Displays information.

Understanding the Worksheet Area

- **Worksheet** A grid of rows and columns.
- **Workbook** A set of worksheets.
- **Cell** The intersection of a row and a column.
- **Cell reference** The column letter and row number of a cell.

Hiding the Status Bar or Formula Bar

1. Click on the View menu.
2. Click on the Formula Bar command to hide the formula bar. Or, click on the Status Bar command to hide the status bar.

Understanding the Screen Display

On your office or home desk, you may have office tools within reach—the phone, a stapler, pens, paper, and so on. Just as you do on your physical desk, Excel keeps a lot of tools close-by on your "electronic" desk. In this chapter, you'll be introduced to some of those tools.

There are three key on-screen elements:

- **Window controls,** which you can use to move, resize, and work with windows.

- **Program window elements,** which enable you to select commands.

- **Worksheet area elements,** which set up the structure of the workbook.

So that you can take advantage of these tools, you should learn what each on-screen element does.

Basic Survival

Understanding the Window Controls

Everything in Windows is displayed in the windows, and each window shares common elements. The following figure identifies the window controls. For information on using these controls, see the next chapter.

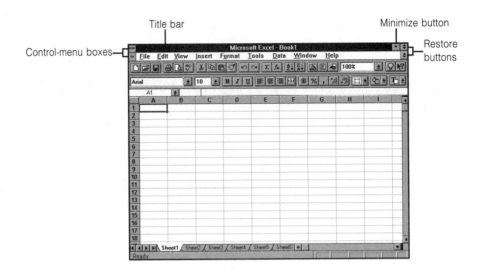

Item	Description
Title bar	Displays the name of the window.
Control-menu box	Provides access to commands for manipulating the window (moving, resizing, closing).
Maximize, Minimize, or Restore buttons	These buttons enable you to change the size of the window.

Understanding the Program Window Elements

Besides the common window control elements, you also see different elements within the program window. These elements are listed in the following table.

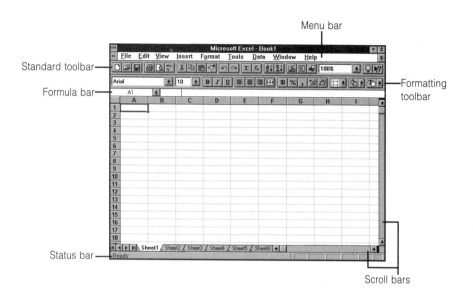

Menu bar

Standard toolbar

Formula bar

Formatting toolbar

Status bar

Scroll bars

Item	Description
Menu bar	Lists the names of the menus. See Chapter 4, "Selecting Menu Commands."
Toolbars	Display buttons that provide quick access to frequently used commands. See Chapter 5, "Using the Toolbars."
Formula bar	Displays the contents of the active cell. To the left of the formula bar, you see the reference area, which contains the cell reference of the current cell. Cell references are described in the next section.
Scroll bars	Enable you to scroll through the window (horizontally and vertically). See Chapter 9, "Moving Around the Worksheet."
Status bar	Displays information about the current worksheet.

Understanding the Worksheet Area

The main part of the Excel screen is the worksheet area. A worksheet is a grid of rows and columns. Rows are numbered from 1 to 16,384; columns are lettered A through IV. (That's a lot of rows and columns—probably more than you'll ever use in one worksheet.)

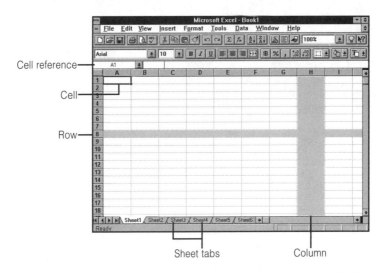

Cell reference

Cell

Row

Sheet tabs   Column

*Cell reference =
column letter,
row number*

The intersection of a column and row is called a *cell*. The cell name or *reference* is made up of the column letter and row number. For instance, A1 is the first cell (column A, row 1). The active cell is indicated by a thick black border. The name of the active cell appears in the reference area next to the formula bar.

In Excel, you can store one set of worksheets in a group, called a *workbook*. Sheet tabs at the bottom of the window show the worksheets; the white tab indicates the current worksheet. You can switch among sheets, add sheets, and rename sheets, and you can have as many sheets as memory allows in a workbook. (See Chapter 19, "Working with Worksheets," for more information on worksheets.) When you save a workbook, all the worksheets within the workbook are saved.

Hiding the Status Bar or Formula Bar

If you decide you want more room for the worksheet area, you can hide the status bar or formula bar. To do so, follow these steps:

1. Point to the View menu and click the left mouse button.

2. Click on the Formula Bar command to hide the formula bar. Click on the Status Bar command to hide the status bar.

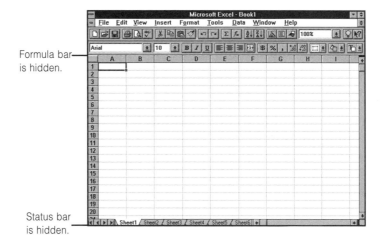

Formula bar is hidden.

Status bar is hidden.

Cheat Sheet

Understanding the Window Controls

▱ Program Control-menu box

▱ Document Control-menu box

▲ Maximize button

▼ Minimize button

⬍ Restore button

Maximizing and Restoring a Window

- To maximize a window, click on the Maximize button ▲ .

    OR

- Select Maximize from the Control menu.

- To restore a window, click on the Restore button ⬍ .

    OR

- Select Restore from the Control menu.

Minimizing a Window

- Click on the Minimize button ▼ .

    OR

- Select Minimize from the Control menu.

Resizing a Window

1. Point to any border or window corner.
2. Hold down the mouse button and drag the border.
3. When the window is the size you want, release the mouse button.

Moving a Window

1. Point to the title bar.
2. Hold down the mouse button and drag the window.
3. When the window is where you want it, release the mouse button.

Working with Windows

Once you start using Microsoft Windows, you will quickly understand why the program is so named: everything in Windows is displayed in a window. For example, program icons are stored in program group windows. Programs open and run in windows. Workbooks are displayed within their own windows in the program window.

Each window has its own set of controls that you can use to resize or move the window.

Basic Survival

Understanding the Window Controls

The window controls appear to the far right and far left of the title bar; these controls look the same and work the same in every Windows program. Therefore, once you learn how to use these controls, you can control windows in any other Windows program.

The following figure identifies the window controls. Note that in this figure, the workbook window appears within the program window and has its own set of controls.

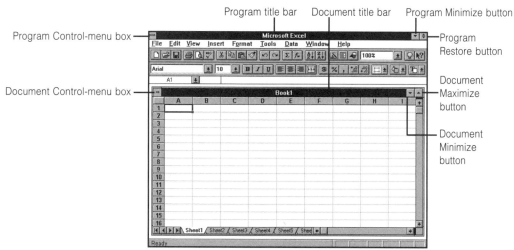

Maximizing and Restoring a Window

You can change the size of a window so that it fills the entire screen or so that it takes up just part of the screen. When a window is as big as it can get, it is *maximized*. When a window is smaller than the entire window, it is *restored*.

When a window is maximized, like the program window in the following figure, it fills the entire screen. A Restore button appears in a maximized window. To restore the window (make it smaller than the entire screen), click the Restore button.

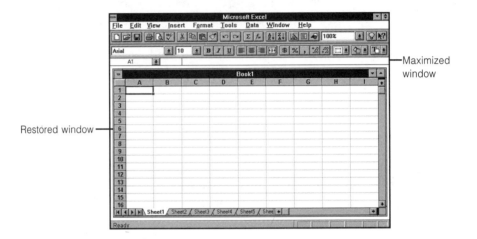

When a window is restored, it has borders and can be moved and resized, like the worksheet window in the preceding figure. Maximize and Minimize buttons appear in restored windows. Click the Maximize button to enlarge the window so that it fills the entire screen.

When you are working on just one worksheet, you will probably want to keep it maximized. When the worksheet window is maximized, it merges with the program window to form one window. You see only one title bar and no borders, and the controls for the worksheet window appear next to the menu bar.

If you are working on several worksheets, you may want to restore them so that you can see part of each worksheet window on-screen. (For more information on working with multiple worksheets, see Chapter 21, "Opening a Workbook.")

Minimizing a Window

You can also minimize a document or program window by clicking on the Minimize button. Doing so shrinks the window to an icon, in effect exiting the program.

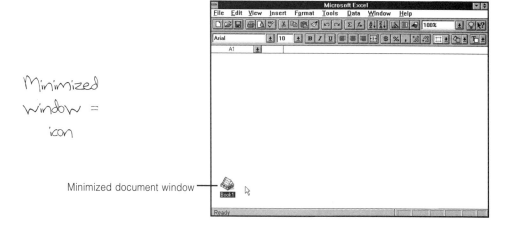

Minimized Window = icon

Minimized document window ———

When you want to restore the icon to a window, simply double-click on the icon.

Beyond Survival

Resizing a Window

When a window is restored (not maximized), you can resize it—make it smaller or larger. By placing the pointer on the top, bottom, left, or right border, you can alter the window's height or width in that direction. To resize the window's height and width at the same time, put the pointer on a window corner. To resize a window, follow these steps:

1. Put the mouse pointer on any border. When the point is in the right spot, the pointer looks like a double-headed arrow.

2. Hold down the mouse button and drag the border to resize the window. You will see an outline of the window as you resize.

3. When the window is the size you want, release the mouse button.

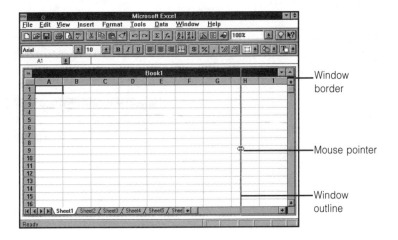

Window border

Mouse pointer

Window outline

Moving a Window

You can also move a window that is restored. For example, you might want to move a window out of the way so you can see other windows. Follow these steps to move a window:

1. Put the mouse pointer on the title bar.

2. Hold down the mouse button and drag the window. As you drag, you see an outline of the window.

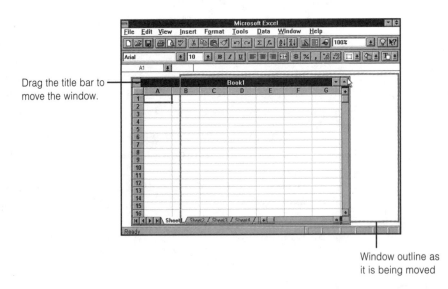

Drag the title bar to move the window.

Window outline as it is being moved

3. When the window is where you want it, release the mouse button.

Cheat Sheet

Selecting a Command

1. Click the menu you want to open.
2. Click the command you want to execute.

Using a Dialog Box

`Edit`	Tab	Click to display options.
`book1.xls`	Text box	Click the text box, and then type the entry.
`16`	Spin box	Click the spin arrows to scroll through values.
(list)	List box	Click an item in the list.
`10`	Drop-down list box	Click the down arrow to see other selections.
(check box)	Check box	Click to turn an option on or off.
(option button)	Option button	Click to turn the option on or off.
`OK`	Command button	Click to execute a command.

Undoing the Last Command

- Select Edit Undo

   OR

- Click the Undo button 🔙.

Using Shortcut Menus

1. Point to the object you want to work with.
2. Click the right mouse button.
3. Click the command you want.

Selecting a Command with the Keyboard

1. Press Alt.
2. Press the selection letter of the menu name.
3. Press the selection letter of the command.

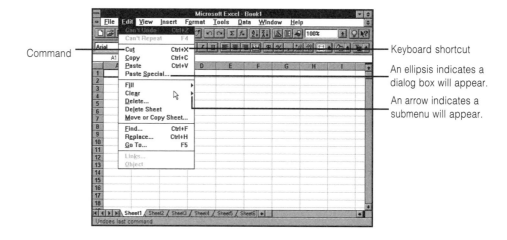

4

Selecting Menu Commands

When you want to tell Excel what to do, you issue a command. However, Excel has too many commands to display on-screen at once, so they are grouped into categories. Each category has its own menu, and the menu names (such as File, Edit, View, and so on) appear in the menu bar along the top of the window. There are many ways to issue a command, but the easiest is to use the mouse.

Basic Survival

Selecting a Command

To select a command, you first open or display the appropriate menu. Then you select the command you want. Follow these steps to select a menu command:

1. Click on the name of the menu you want to open. For example, click on the Edit menu to see commands that are related to editing. The menu drops down, and you see a list of commands.

Command —

Keyboard shortcut

An ellipsis indicates a dialog box will appear.

An arrow indicates a submenu will appear.

2. Click on the command you want to execute. Some commands are executed right away. However, when you select some commands, you see a submenu of options; click on the one you want. Still other commands display a dialog box so that you can select options for the command. For instance, when you issue the Print command to print a worksheet, the Print dialog box appears. Here you tell Excel such things as how many copies to print or which pages to print. The next section explains how to make selections in a dialog box.

Remember!

To close a menu without making a selection, click on the menu name again, click outside the menu, or press the Esc key.

Using a Dialog Box

If Excel needs additional information about the command (for instance, when printing, Excel needs to know how many copies to print), you see a dialog box. Dialog boxes include options for you to choose from. Even though every dialog box is different, they all share common elements. If you learn how to use these elements, you will be able to use any dialog box you encounter.

Some dialog boxes have more than one set of options. In this case, the sets of options are indicated by tabs at the top of the dialog box. You can click on the tab to display the appropriate set of options.

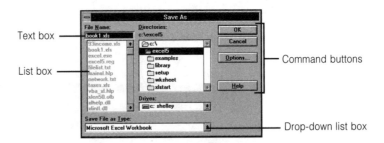

22

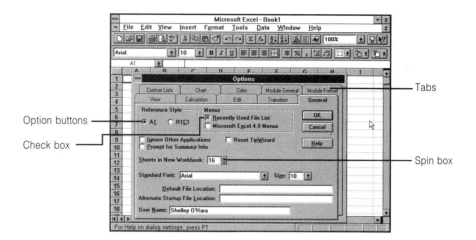

Option buttons

Check box

Tabs

Spin box

The following table explains how to select or activate each type of
option.

Icon	Description
Edit	**Tab** Click on the tab name to display the options for that tab.
book1.xls	**Text box** Click in the text box, and then type the entry. If the text box already contains an entry, you can drag across it to select it, and then press Delete to delete it.
16	**Spin box** A spin box is a type of text box with two arrows next to it. You can type an entry in the spin box, just as you do for a text box, or you can click the spin arrows to scroll through the text box values.

continues

23

Icon	Description
	List box A list box displays a list of selections. Click on the item you want in the list.
10	**Drop-down list box** A drop-down list box displays only the first selection in a list. Click on the down arrow next to the item to display other selections. Then click on the item you want.
Menus ☒ Recently Used File List ☐ Microsoft Excel 4.0 Menus	**Check box** Click the check box to turn the option on or off. If the check box has an X in it, it is selected. Clicking the box again turns the option off. If the check box is empty, the option is not selected. If a dialog box has more than one check box, you can check as many check boxes as you want.
Reference Style ⦿ A1 ○ R1C1	**Option button** Click in the option button to toggle the option on (it appears darkened) or off (it appears blank). You can select only one option button in each group of option buttons.
OK	**Command button** Click a command button to execute a command. The OK command button confirms and carries out the command. The Cancel button cancels the command. The Help command button displays help about the current dialog box. Some dialog boxes also have other buttons that, when selected, display other dialog boxes. These buttons have ellipses on them (just like menu commands that display dialog boxes).

Beyond Survival

Undoing the Last Command

The command you will probably value the most in Excel is the Undo command. You can use this command to undo the most recent action you performed. For instance, if you deleted some data accidentally, choose the Undo command to undo the deletion. You can undo most editing and formatting changes. You cannot undo saves, scrolling, and some other commands. If Undo is dimmed, you cannot undo the most recent operation.

Ctrl + Z To Undo

If you realize immediately you want to undo something, follow these steps:

1. Click on Edit in the menu bar.

2. Click on the Undo command. Excel undoes the last action you performed.

If you'd rather use the toolbar, you can simply click .

Repeating a Command

If you need to perform the same command two or three times in a row, you can repeat it. For instance, suppose that you changed the font size for selected cells, and then you selected another group of cells and needed to make the same changes. Rather than select the same commands again, use the Repeat command to make the same font size changes to other entries. Follow these steps:

F4 To Repeat

1. Click on the Edit menu.

2. Select the Repeat command. Excel repeats the last command.

You can also click on the Repeat button ⟳ in the Standard toolbar.

Using Shortcut Menus

Opening a menu, selecting a command, entering dialog box options, and choosing OK can get tiresome. Excel provides some shortcut menus that make commands just a mouse click away.

To display a shortcut menu, follow these steps:

1. Point to the object you what you want to work with. You can point to the worksheet area, to the toolbar, or to an object.

2. Click the right mouse button. Excel displays a shortcut menu with

25

commands that are related to the selected object. For instance, if you display the shortcut menu for the toolbar, you will see options for displaying other toolbars or customizing the toolbar.

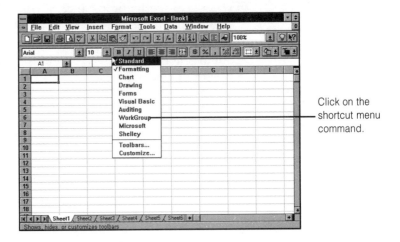

Click on the shortcut menu command.

3. Click on the command you want from the shortcut menu. Excel carries out the command.

Selecting a Command with the Keyboard

If you like to keep your hands on the keyboard, you may want to use the keyboard to select menu commands. To use the keyboard, follow these steps:

1. Press Alt to activate the menu bar.

2. Press the selection letter of the menu name. The selection letter is the letter that appears underlined on-screen (for example, the F in File).

Selection letter —

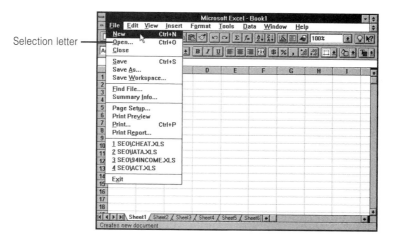

Key combinations have plus signs—like ATT + F

3. Press the selection letter of the command.

4. If a dialog box appears, make selections as follows:

To Select	Do This
Tab	Press Ctrl+PgUp or Ctrl+PgDn to cycle through the tabs.
Text box	Press Tab to move to the text box; then type the entry.
Spin box	Press Tab to move to the spin box. Press ↑ to cycle forward through the increments. Press ↓ to cycle backwards through the increments.
List box	Press Tab to move to the list box. Use ↑ and ↓ to highlight an item in the list.
Drop-down list box	Press Tab to move to the drop-down list, press ↓ to display the list, and then use ↑ or ↓ to select an item in the list.
Check box	Press and hold Alt, and then press the selection letter for the check box.

continues

To Select	Do This
Option button	Press and hold Alt, and then press the selection letter for the option.
Command button	Press Enter or click OK. Press Esc or click Cancel. For other buttons, press Alt+the selection letter.

Using Keyboard Shortcuts

Another way to select commands from the keyboard is to use the shortcut keys. Shortcut keys appear in the menus next to the command names. A shortcut key is often a key combination: press and hold down the first key, press the second key, and then release both. Here are a few of the most useful shortcut keys:

Command	Keyboard Shortcut	Description
Bold	Ctrl+B	Makes the selected text bold.
Italic	Ctrl+I	Underlines the selected text.
Underline	Ctrl+U	Makes the selected text italic.
Undo	Ctrl+Z	Undoes the most recent command.
File Save	Ctrl+S	Saves the current file.
File Open	Ctrl+O	Opens a previously saved file.

Cheat Sheet

Viewing the Button Names

- Point to the tool (don't click the mouse button).
- If ToolTips are turned off, select View Toolbars and click the Show ToolTips check box.

Using the Toolbars

- Click the button you want to use.
- If there is a ↓ button to the right, click it to display a list box. Then click on the option you want.

Displaying and Hiding a Toolbar

1. Select View Toolbars.
2. Check the toolbar(s) you want to display.
3. Uncheck the toolbar(s) you want to hide.
4. Click on OK.

5

Using the Toolbars

As you work in Excel, you will realize that you use the same commands and features over and over. To make it easy to select these common commands, Excel includes buttons for them. These buttons display little pictures representing the command and are grouped into two sets or two toolbars: the Standard toolbar and the Formatting toolbar. You can use the buttons in the toolbars to quickly access a feature or command.

Basic Survival

Viewing the Button Names

A picture is used on each button to indicate its function, but sometimes the picture isn't enough. To find out what a button does, place the mouse pointer on the bottom edge of the button. The button name appears under the button, and a description of the tool appears in the status bar.

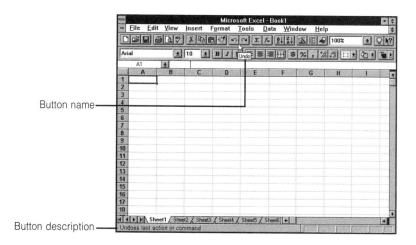

Button name

Button description

You might need to move the mouse around to get the pointer in the right spot to display the ToolTip. If you can't get this to work, check to be sure that ToolTips are turned on. Select the View Toolbars command to access the Toolbars dialog box, and make sure there is an X in the Show ToolTips check box. Click OK.

Using the Toolbars

To use a toolbar button, point to the appropriate button. Then click the mouse button once. Excel carries out the selected command or feature.

If a button has a down arrow next to it, click on the arrow to display a list of options. To select an option from the list, click on the option you want.

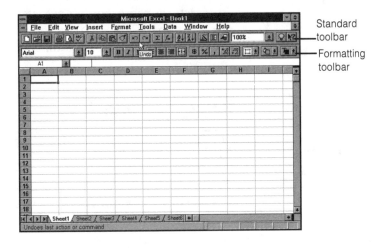

Standard toolbar

Formatting toolbar

Using the Standard Toolbar

The Standard toolbar includes buttons for working with files, cutting and copying text, undoing and redoing commands, and more. The following table identifies each button and its purpose:

Button	Name	Description
	New Workbook	Creates a new workbook
	Open	Opens a previously saved file
	Save	Saves the workbook
	Print	Prints the workbook currently on-screen

Button	Name	Description
	Print Preview	Changes to print preview
	Spelling	Starts the Speller
	Cut	Cuts selected range to Clipboard
	Copy	Copies selected range to Clipboard
	Paste	Pastes data from Clipboard
	Format Painter	Copies formatting
	Undo	Undoes last command
	Repeat	Repeats last command
	AutoSum	Creates a sum function
	FunctionWizard	Starts the FunctionWizard
	Sort Ascending	Sorts selection in ascending order
	Sort Descending	Sorts selection in descending order
	ChartWizard	Starts the ChartWizard
	Text Box	Creates a text box
	Drawing	Displays the Drawing toolbar
	Zoom Control	Enables you to zoom the worksheet to percent you specify
	TipWizard	Starts the TipWizard
	Help	Enables you to get context-sensitive help

Using the Formatting Toolbar

The Formatting toolbar provides buttons for formatting your data—making entries bold, changing the font, and so on. The following table identifies the buttons in this toolbar.

Button	Name	Description
`Arial`	Font	Enables you to select the font from a drop-down list
`10`	Font Size	Enables you to select a font size from a drop-down list
B	Bold	Applies bold to selected range.
I	Italic	Applies italic to selected range
U	Underline	Underlines selected range
	Align Left	Aligns selected range to the left
	Center	Centers selected range
	Align Right	Aligns selected range to the right
	Center Across Columns	Centers text across selected columns
$	Currency Style	Applies currency style to the selected range
%	Percent Style	Applies percent style to the selected range
,	Comma Style	Applies comma style to the selected range
	Increase Decimal	Increases the number of decimal points displayed in the selected range
	Decrease Decimal	Decreases the number of decimal points displayed in the selected range

Button	Name	Description
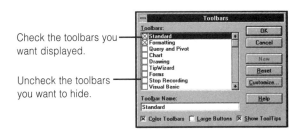 Borders	Borders	Enables you to select and apply borders to selected range
Color	Color	Enables you to select and apply color to selected range
Font Color	Font Color	Enables you to select and apply color to text in selected range

Beyond Survival

Displaying and Hiding a Toolbar

If you don't use the toolbars, you may want to turn them off so that you have more room on-screen for the worksheet. You can also display other toolbars.

Follow these steps to display and hide toolbars:

1. Click on View in the menu bar. The View menu appears.

2. Click on the Toolbars command. You see the Toolbars dialog box.

Check the toolbars you want displayed.

Uncheck the toolbars you want to hide.

3. Uncheck the toolbar(s) that you want to hide by clicking the appropriate check box.

4. Click on the check box(es) for the toolbar(s) you want to display.

5. Click on OK.

Cheat Sheet

Using Help Contents

1. Click Help Contents.
2. Click the topic you want.
3. Click the next topic you want.
4. Continue clicking on topics until a How To window appears.

Navigating Through the Help System

- Click Back to go to the previous topic.
- Click History for a list of all the topics you viewed.
- Click Contents to return to the Help Contents screen.
- Click Index to use the index.
- Click Search to search for a help topic.
- Double-click the Control-menu box to close the Help window.

Searching for Help

1. Select Help Search.
2. In the text box, type name of the topic you want to find.
3. In the list that is displayed, click the topic you want.
4. Click the Show Topics button.
5. Click the topic you want.
6. Click the Go To button.

Getting Context-Sensitive Help

- Click the Help button , and then click the on-screen item or command you need help with.
- Click the Help button in a dialog box or press F1.

Getting Help

If you can't remember how to perform a task, use Excel's on-line help system to remind you. The on-line help system offers many ways to get help. You can look through the Contents screen to find the topic you want—just as you would scan the table of contents of a book. You can also look through the Index or search through the help system for the topic you want.

Basic Survival

Using Help Contents

Using Help Contents is like using the table of contents of a book. When you use this command, Excel displays a list of topics. You select the topic you want, and Excel displays additional subtopics. You continue selecting topics until you find the information you want.

To use Help Contents, follow these steps:

1. Click on Help in the menu bar.

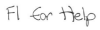

2. Click on the Contents command. You see the Microsoft Excel Help Contents window. Help topics are grouped into five major categories.

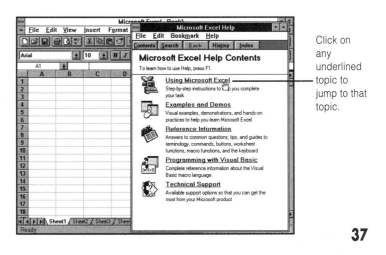

Click on any underlined topic to jump to that topic.

3. **Click on the topic you want.** For instance, if you want step-by-step information on using Excel, click on Using Microsoft Excel. If you want Reference information (for example, information about worksheet functions), click on Reference Information.

Click on
green under-
lined Topics
To jump To
Them

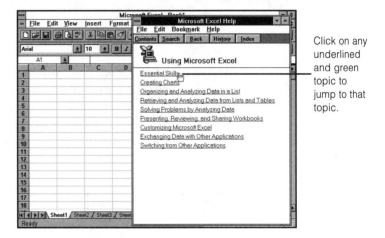

Click on any
underlined
and green
topic to
jump to that
topic.

4. **Click on the next topic you want.** More subtopics are displayed.

5. **Continue clicking on topics** until the How To window appears. The How To window lists the steps you follow to complete the task.

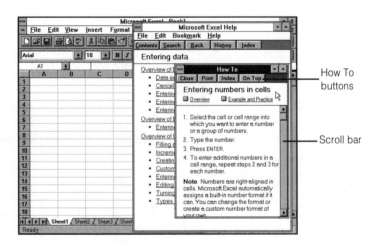

How To
buttons

Scroll bar

The How To window is a separate window with its own scroll bars, buttons, and window controls. You can do any of the following:

- To scroll through the window, click on the up or down scroll arrows or drag the scroll box.

- To close the How To window, double-click the Control-menu box or click on the Close button.

- To print the how-to information, click the Print button.

- To display an index of topics, click the Index button (see the section "Using the Help Index" in this chapter).

- To return to the document and keep the How To window displayed, click the On Top button.

- A dotted line under an Excel word or phrase means that if you click on it, a pop-up definition for the term will be displayed. After you click on the term and read the definition, click back in the How To window to close the definition.

Navigating Through the Help System

Getting to the steps you need may not be easy. When you are jumping from topic to topic, you may feel as if you are lost in a maze. The buttons across the top of the screen in the Help window can help you move around among the topics:

Back	Click the Back button to go back to the previous topic.
History	To move to an earlier topic, click the History button. You see all the topics you have selected so far. Click on the topic you want to jump to.
Contents	To return to the opening Help Contents screen, click the Contents button.
Index	To use the Index, click the Index button. See the section "Using the Help Index," next.
Search	To search for a help topic, click the Search button. See the section "Searching for Help."
▭	To close the help window, double-click on the Control-menu box.

Beyond Survival

Using the Help Index

If you don't like searching through the selected topic categories, you can use the Index to find help. Using the Index, you can display all topics that start with a certain letter. You can then jump to the topic you want.

Follow these steps:

1. Click on Help in the menu bar.

2. Click on the Index command. The Index appears.

3. Click on the first letter of the topic you need help with. For instance, to list all help topics that start with C, click on C.

4. Click on the topic you want. You will see help information on the selected topic. Scroll through and read the steps.

Double-click Control-menu box To close Help

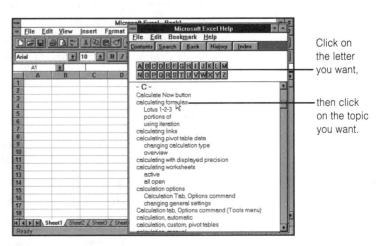

Click on the letter you want,

then click on the topic you want.

5. When you are finished, close each help window by double-clicking on its Control-menu box.

Searching for Help

Sometimes jumping from topic to topic in the Index is time consuming and leads you down a blind alley. Therefore, there might be times when you want to type in a particular topic name instead of trying to figure out what Excel might have indexed it under. Excel will match what you type to its list (a different list than appears in the Index), and will show you the topics that pertain to the item. Then you can quickly jump to the appropriate help window.

Follow these steps to search for a particular help topic:

1. Click on Help in the menu bar.

2. Click on the Search for Help on command.

3. In the Search dialog box, type the topic you want to find. You can type all or part of the topic. Excel displays matching topics.

4. Click on the topic you want from the list.

5. Click on the Show Topics button. Excel displays the available topics related to the topic you selected in step 4.

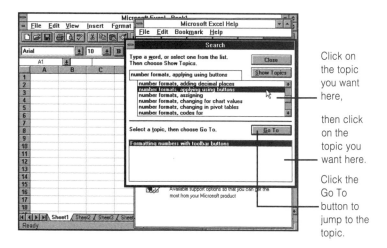

Click on the topic you want here,

then click on the topic you want here.

Click the Go To button to jump to the topic.

6. Click on the topic you want.

7. Click on the Go To button. Excel displays the pertinent help screen.

Getting Context-Sensitive Help

If you want help about a particular command, window element, or dialog box, you can ask Excel to display context-sensitive help—that is, help about the selected item. To do so, use one of these three methods:

- To get help on a particular on-screen element, click on the Help button. Notice that the mouse pointer changes to a question mark and an arrow. Then click on the item for which you want help. For instance, you can click the Help button and then click the scroll bar in the document window to get help on scrolling through the window.

- To get help on a particular command, click on the Help button, open the menu that contains the command on which you want help, and then click on the command. Excel displays pertinent help.

- To get help on a dialog box, click the Help button in the dialog box or press F1. Excel displays help information relating to the current dialog box.

Using the TipWizard

Another help feature you can use is the TipWizard. When the TipWizard is on, a special toolbar is displayed. It gives you helpful hints and shortcuts about commands and features as you use them.

To use TipWizard, follow these steps:

1. Click on the TipWizard button ![button]. The TipWizard toolbar appears.

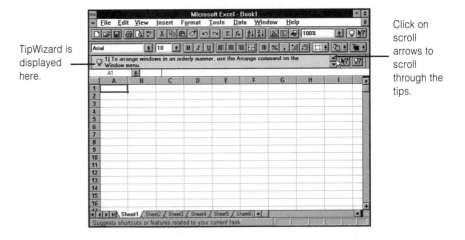

TipWizard is displayed here.

Click on scroll arrows to scroll through the tips.

2. Click on the scroll arrows to scroll through the tips.

3. Click the TipWizard button again to turn off this feature.

Cheat Sheet

Exiting Excel

1. Save all workbooks that you have created.
2. Select File Exit.

Exiting Windows

1. In Program Manager, select File Exit Windows.
2. In the dialog box, click OK.

7

Exiting Excel

When you are finished working on your worksheet, you should save the worksheet, exit Excel, exit Windows, and turn off the computer. (You should do all four in that order.) If you forget to save, Excel will remind you with a dialog box. (Saving is covered in Chapter 20, "Saving and Closing a Workbook.") If you try to exit Windows without exiting Excel, you'll be reminded to save your work also.

Basic Survival

Exiting Excel

When you are finished working in Excel, you can exit the program and return to the Program Manager. From here, you can start another program or exit Windows and turn off the computer.

Follow these steps to exit Excel:

1. Save all workbooks that you have created. Chapter 20, "Saving and Closing a Workbook," explains how to save your work. If you try to exit without saving, you will see a dialog box prompting you to save.

2. Click on the File menu. You will see a list of file-related commands.

3. Click on the Exit command. You return to the Microsoft Windows Program Manager. From here, you can start another program or exit Windows.

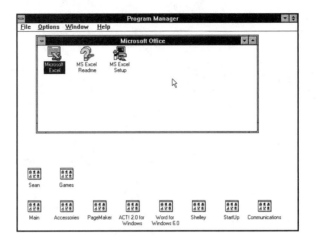

Exiting Windows

If you are done working with the computer and want to turn it off, you need to first exit Windows. Windows needs to take care of some "housekeeping" chores before it closes. If you turn off the computer without exiting Windows, these chores aren't completed, and you could encounter problems with Windows later or lose some data.

To exit Windows, follow these steps:

1. In Program Manager, click on the File menu.

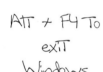

2. Click on the Exit Windows command. You see the Exit Windows dialog box, asking you whether you want to exit Windows.

3. Click OK. You return to DOS, and the prompt C:\> appears on-screen.

PART 2

Creating a Worksheet

You can create a worksheet for any purpose you want: to total sales, to track business expenses, to manage a budget. No matter what type of worksheet you want to create, you follow the same steps. Part 2 covers how to create a worksheet—how to enter text, numbers, and formulas, and how to work with the data you enter. In particular, this part covers the following topics:

- Planning your Worksheet
- Moving Around the Worksheet
- Entering Text, Numbers, and Dates
- Selecting a Range
- Entering Formulas
- Entering Functions
- Editing Data
- Deleting Data
- Moving Data
- Copying Data
- Filling Data
- Working with Worksheets
- Saving and Closing a Workbook
- Opening a Workbook

Cheat Sheet

Planning the Worksheet

1. Define the purpose or goal of the worksheet.
2. Figure out which values you need to enter manually and which values can be calculated by formulas.
3. Sketch out the worksheet on paper.

Creating the Worksheet

1. Type the text entries.
2. Enter the numeric values.
3. Create the formulas.
4. Save the worksheet.

Formatting and Printing the Worksheet

1. Decide how you want your information to be displayed on the spreadsheet.
2. Change the formatting of cells and cell ranges.
3. Save your worksheet after editing.
4. Print it out.

Checking the Worksheet

1. Calculate formulas with a hand-held calculator.
2. Double check cell references.
3. Spell check the worksheet.
4. Check formulas with Excel's auditing feature.
5. If explanations are needed, add notes to the appropriate cells.
6. Save the worksheet again.

8

Planning Your Worksheet

Before you start entering data and formulas, it's a good idea to take some time to plan your worksheet. Planning a worksheet offers these benefits:

- You have a good understanding of what you want the worksheet to accomplish. You know which values you need to enter manually and which are calculated.

- By sketching out the organization first, you avoid redoing the worksheet, and you won't have to do as much moving and rearranging.

- You can determine the best way to complete the worksheet, considering which data entry techniques you can take advantage of. For instance, if you are entering a series of months, you can use the Fill feature instead of typing them all. You can simply enter the first month and select a specific command that fills in the names of the rest of the months in the following cells. (See Chapter 18, "Filling Data," for more on this feature.)

- You can check for accuracy to verify that the worksheet results are correct.

SkeTch The worksheeT on paper firsT!

Basic Survival

Planning the Worksheet

The first step in planning the worksheet is defining the purpose of the worksheet. Ask yourself, "What is the goal? What do I want to accomplish? What questions will the worksheet answer?" Knowing what you want from the outset will help you create a worksheet that solves a problem or answers a question—instead of one that just includes a lot of numbers.

You might decide that the worksheet will track sales by division or keep track of budget costs. Once you *know* the purpose, you can figure out how to achieve that purpose.

The second step is to figure out what values you will need to enter and what values will be calculated by formulas.

The final planning step is to sketch out the worksheet on paper. This paper version will help you as you create the worksheet on-screen.

Creating the Worksheet

After you create a solid plan, you'll be ready to create the worksheet. (The chapters in Part 2 will help you get started.) Here's a good plan for creating the worksheet:

1. Type the text entries: the column and row headings, the worksheet titles, and any other text information. This text information provides the framework for the values. See Chapter 10, "Entering Text, Numbers, and Dates," for details.

2. Enter the numeric values. Numeric values can include numbers or dates and times. Don't worry yet about how the numbers appear on-screen. It's easier to *format* (change the way they look) after you enter all the numbers. See Chapter 10, "Entering Text, Numbers, and Dates," for more information.

3. Create the formulas. Keep in mind that in some cases you can create one formula and then copy this formula across the worksheet. For instance, you may have a formula that sums a column of quarter 1 sales. If you also want to sum the sales for

quarters 2, 3, and 4, you can copy the same formula. Creating formulas is discussed in Chapter 12, "Entering Formulas." Copying is covered in Chapter 17, "Copying Data."

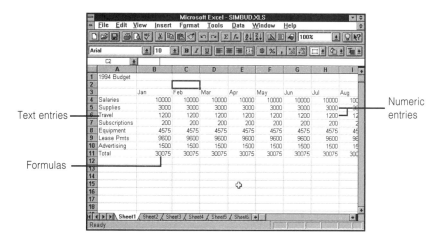

Save often!

4. Save the worksheet. You need to save the worksheet not just when you have completed it, but periodically as you build it. If something happens to the power, and you haven't saved, you will lose all your hard work. Therefore, it's a good idea to save every 5 or 10 minutes. You'll learn about saving in Chapter 20, "Saving and Closing a Workbook."

Formatting and Printing the Worksheet

After you are sure the values and text are okay, you can spend some time making the information look nice. Excel offers a wide range of formatting features, including the following:

- Change the number format that is used; for instance, the Currency number format displays the number 1200.98 as $1,200.98. (You don't have to type the dollar sign or the comma.)

- Make cell contents bold, italic, or underlined.

- Add a border or shade to a cell or range of cells.

- Change the font and font size for the worksheet title or worksheet headings.

- Change the alignment of data in cells.

- Display key information in a different color.

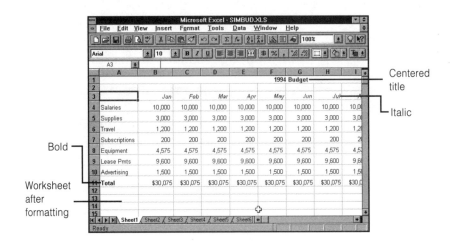

Centered title

Italic

Bold

Worksheet after formatting

These are just some of the formatting features available. For more information, see Part 3 of this book, which discusses formatting.

Once the worksheet is set up the way you want it, you can print it, as described in Chapter 34, "Printing a Workbook."

Checking the Worksheet

Avoid spelling errors by running the spell checker

After you complete the worksheet, it's a good idea to check the printout and check the formulas. Calculate the formulas with a hand-held calculator. You don't have to worry about Excel making a mathematical mistake, but you need to be sure that you've entered the formulas correctly. If you refer to a wrong cell or enter a wrong value, the formula may not be calculated as you intended it to be. Cross checking helps avoid any errors.

Several features that are covered in Part 4 of this book are handy when checking the worksheet. For example, you can use Excel's speller to check for spelling errors. See Chapter 41, "Checking Spelling."

Cheat Sheet

Moving to a Cell

- With the mouse, click on the cell you want.
- With the keyboard, use the arrow keys or key combinations.

Scrolling the Worksheet

- The worksheet's scroll bars work like the scroll bars in any window.
- The active cell doesn't change when you scroll to a different part of the worksheet.

Moving to a Specific Cell

1. Select Edit Go To.
2. Type the cell reference in the Reference text box.
3. Click OK.

Moving to a Different Sheet

- Click on the sheet tab at the bottom of the workbook window.

9

Moving Around the Worksheet

The Excel worksheet contains 16,000 rows and 256 columns. You probably won't use that much space, but you do need a way to move around within the area of the worksheet you will use. You can easily move from cell to cell and from sheet to sheet with Excel.

Basic Survival

Moving to a Cell

In Excel, the active cell is indicated by a thick black border. When you type data or enter a formula, that entry will be placed in the *active cell*. If you want the entry to go into another cell, you need to move to that cell first.

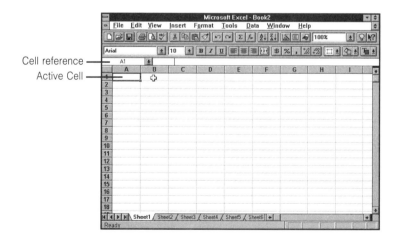

Cell reference

Active Cell

To move around the worksheet, you can use the mouse or the keyboard. At first, the mouse may be easier to use. To move with the mouse, point to the cell you want. Notice that the mouse pointer appears as a thick cross when within the worksheet area. When the pointer is on the cell you want, click the mouse button. That cell becomes the active cell, and the cell reference for the active cell appears in the reference area.

Once you become more comfortable with Excel, you may prefer to keep your hands on the keyboard. To move with the keyboard, use the arrow keys and key combinations listed in the following table.

Press	To move...
→	Right one cell.
←	Left one cell.
↓	Down one cell.
↑	Up one cell.
Ctrl+→	To the right edge of the current region.
Ctrl+←	To the left edge of the current region.
Ctrl+↓	To the bottom edge of the current region.
Ctrl+↑	To the top edge of the current region.
Home	First cell in the row.
Ctrl+Home	First cell in the worksheet.
Ctrl+End	Lower right cell in the worksheet.
PgDn	Down one screen.
PgUp	Up one screen.
Alt+PgDn	Right one screen.
Alt+PgUp	Left one screen.
Ctrl+PgDn	To the next worksheet.
Ctrl+PgUp	To the previous worksheet.

Scrolling the Worksheet

If you want to keep the active cell where it is, but view another part of the worksheet, use the scroll arrows along the right and bottom sides of the workbook window. Click on the scroll arrow in the direction you want to move, or drag the scroll box.

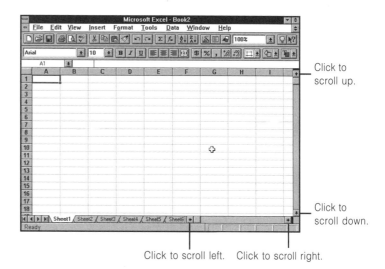

Click to scroll up.

Click to scroll down.

Click to scroll left.   Click to scroll right.

Active cell doesn'T change when you scroll

If you scroll the worksheet, keep in mind that the active cell doesn't change. If you type an entry, it will be entered in the active cell, which may not be the cell you're looking at or that you think you're in. If you scroll and then want to select a cell, be sure to point to the cell you want and click the mouse button.

Beyond Survival

Moving to a Specific Cell

Moving from cell to cell with the mouse, keyboard, or scroll bars is fine when you want to move a short distance. But if you want to move a greater distance, you might want to investigate the Go To command. This command enables you to move quickly to any cell in the worksheet.

To use the Go To command, follow these steps:

1. Select the Edit Go To command. The Go To dialog box appears.

2. In the Reference text box, type the cell reference that you want to go to.

F5 = Go To

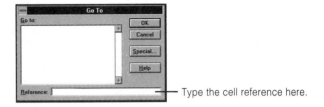

Type the cell reference here.

3. Click OK. Excel moves to the selected cell.

Moving to a Different Sheet

In addition to rows and columns, each workbook includes several worksheets. Think of these worksheets as a single piece of paper in a pad. You can set up many separate worksheets on each workbook, and each worksheet is indicated with a tab at the bottom of the workbook window.

When you start Excel, Sheet1 is selected. If you want to work with just one sheet, you can just enter data on that sheet. If you want to work with additional worksheets, you need to select the sheet you want first. To make a different worksheet active, click on the sheet tab at the bottom of the workbook window. The active tab appears in white.

Ctrl + PgDn = go To next sheet

Ctrl + PgUp = go To preceding sheet

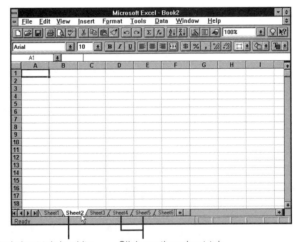

The selected sheet tab is white.

Click another sheet tab to move to another sheet.

Cheat Sheet

Entering Text and Numbers

1. Select the cell you want.
2. Type the text or number.
3. Press Enter to accept the entry.

Entering Dates and Times

1. Select the cell you want.
2. Type the date or time using a predefined format.
3. Press Enter.

Entering Decimal Places Automatically

1. Select Tools Options.
2. Click the Edit tab.
3. Check the Fixed Decimal check box.
4. If necessary, enter a new value in the Places spin box.
5. Click OK.

10

Entering Text, Numbers, and Dates

You can enter two types of entries in an Excel worksheet: values and
formulas. *Values* include numbers, text, dates, and times. Values are
unchanging; that is, once you enter a value it stays as it was entered
unless you change it. *Formulas* are calculated based on the values you
enter. If you change a value referenced in a formula, the formula is
updated to reflect the change. Chapter 12 covers how to create a
formula.

Basic Survival

Entering Text

Without text, your worksheet will just be a jumble of numbers. You
usually enter text for the column and row headings or for product
names or other text entries. Entering text is simple. Just follow these
steps:

1. Select the cell you want.

2. Type the text. You can type up to 255 characters in a cell. As you
type any entry of text, numbers, or formulas, Excel displays a
Confirm button (a check mark) and a Cancel button (an X) next to
the entry in the formula bar.

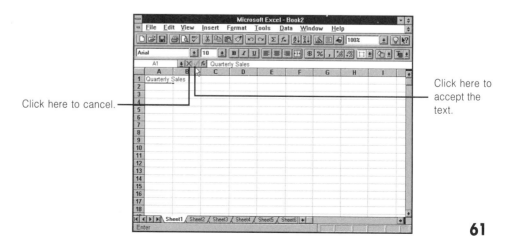

Click here to cancel.

Click here to
accept the
text.

3. Click the Confirm button or press Enter to accept the entry. Excel enters the text and moves to the next cell. Alternatively, you can press any arrow key to accept the entry and move the cell pointer to the next cell in that direction. (If you want to cancel the entry, click the Cancel button or press Esc.)

Note that if the text entry is too long, it will spill over to the cells next to it (unless those cells contain data). If the cells contain data, the displayed entry will be truncated; the actual entry is still intact, you just can't see it. To see all of the entry, you need to widen the column or wrap the text. (See Chapter 23, "Aligning Data," and Chapter 24, "Changing the Number Format," for more information.)

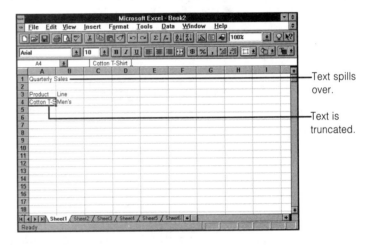

Text spills over.

Text is truncated.

By default, text entries are left-aligned. You can change the alignment as described in Chapter 23, "Aligning Data." You can also change the font and other cell formats (see Chapter 22, "Formatting Data," for more information).

Entering Numbers

The reason you create a worksheet is most likely to work with and manipulate numbers: sales numbers, business expenses, budget amounts, and so on. Numbers are the heart and soul of a worksheet. In an Excel worksheet, you can enter positive and negative numbers with which to calculate (add, subtract, multiply, and so on).

To enter a number, follow these steps:

1. Select the cell into which you want to enter a number.

2. Type the number. To type a negative number, precede the number with a minus sign or enclose the number in parentheses. As you type the entry, Excel displays a Confirm button and a Cancel button next to the entry in the formula bar.

3. Click the Confirm button or press Enter to accept the entry. If you want to cancel the entry, click the Cancel button or press Esc. Excel enters the text and moves to the next cell. You can also press any arrow key to make the entry and move the cell pointer to the next cell in that direction.

If the number is too big to fit within the cell, Excel displays the number using scientific notation. If you want to see the whole number, you can change the number format or widen the column. (See Chapter 24, "Changing the Number Format," and Chapter 25, "Changing the Column Width," for more information.)

By default, numbers are right-aligned and are displayed in the General number format, but you can change both of those attributes if you want. You can also type commas, percent signs, dollar signs, and a period (to indicate decimal places) as you type the entry. Excel will automatically use the appropriate format (for example, if you type 2,000, Excel will use the comma format).

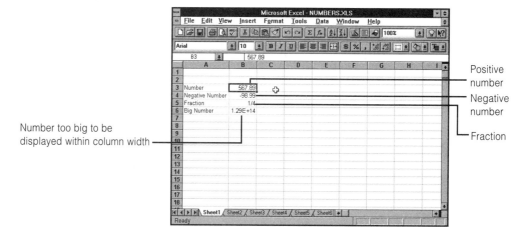

To enter a fraction, type 0 plus the fraction. For instance, to enter 1/4, type 0 1/4. If you type 1/4, Excel thinks you are entering a date.

Beyond Survival

Entering Dates and Times

Using dates you can keep track of when an expense was incurred, when a project was completed, when a bill was sent, and so on. Dates are useful in worksheets because you can use them in calculations. You can, for example, create an aging report on past due bills by using date calculations.

Current date — Ctrl + ;

Follow these steps to enter a date:

1. Select the cell you want.

2. Type the date using one of these formats:

4/4/94

4-Apr-94

4-Apr (assumes current year)

Apr-4 (assumes current year)

3. Press Enter. No matter how you enter the date, you should see the date in the formula bar in this format: 4/4/1994.

If the entry appears as text in the formula bar, Excel does not think the entry is a date or time. Be sure to use one of the above formats. On the other hand, if you are entering a number that's not a date and it appears as a date, it may be that the cell has a date format. Check the cell format. (See Chapter 22, "Formatting Data.")

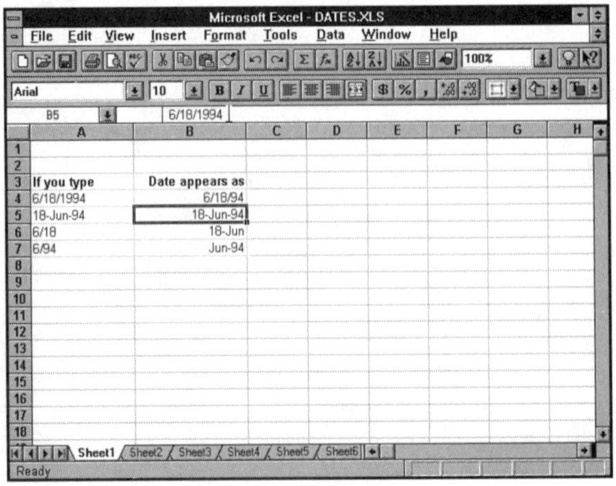

You can enter the time to keep track of when a project started and ended or to timestamp when a bill was paid. To enter a time, follow these steps:

1. Select the cell you want.

Current Time—Ctrl + Shift + :

2. Type the time using one of these formats:

   9:45

   9:45 PM

   9:45:55 PM

   21:45

   21:45:55

3. Press Enter.

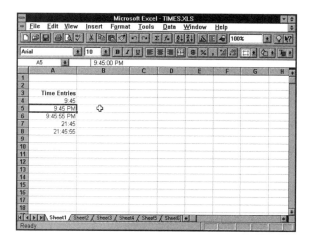

Excel keeps track of dates by assigning each date a serial number, starting with the first day in the century. No matter how the date appears in the cell, Excel thinks of the date as this serial number. Because Excel thinks of dates in terms of serial numbers, you can use dates in calculations. For instance, you can subtract two dates to find out the number of days between the two.

Excel keeps track of times by storing them as a fractional part of 24 hours. Again, this enables you to create calculations with times (adding two times, for instance).

Cheat Sheet

Selecting a Range with the Mouse

1. Click the first cell in the range.
2. Drag across the cells you want to include.

Selecting a Range with the Keyboard

1. With the arrow keys, move to the first cell in the range.
2. Hold down Shift.
3. Highlight the range with the arrow keys.

Selection Shortcuts

To Select	Do This
A column	Click the column letter.
A row	Click the row number.
The entire worksheet	Click the Select All button.

Selecting a Noncontiguous Range

1. Select the first range.
2. Hold down Ctrl and select the next range.

11

Selecting a Range

When you want to select an individual cell, you just click on it. This method works fine when you want to work with a single cell, but there will be times when you want to work with a group of cells. For instance, you may want to copy a group of cells, or you may want to delete a group of cells.

In Excel, a group of cells is called a *range*; a range can be a group of cells next to each other, an entire row, an entire column, a group of cells in one area and another group of cells in another area (called a noncontiguous range), or the entire worksheet. Selecting a cell or range is the equivalent of telling Excel, "This is what I want to work on."

Basic Survival

Selecting a Range with the Mouse

The easiest way to select a range is to use the mouse. Most often, the ranges you select will be next to each other, so selecting a range is as simple as dragging across the cells you want. Follow these steps:

1. Click on the first cell in the range.

2. Hold down the mouse button and drag across the cells you want to include.

3. Release the mouse button. The range appears highlighted on-screen.

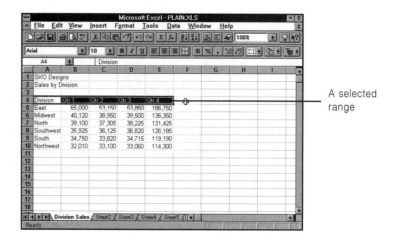

A selected range

A range is indicated with a range reference, which includes the upper-left cell reference, a colon, and the lower-right cell reference. The range A1:B3, for instance, includes these cells A1, B1, A2, B2, A3, and B3.

To deselect a range, click outside of the selected range.

Selecting a Range with the Keyboard

If you prefer to keep your hands on the keyboard while working, you can select a range without reaching for the mouse. Follow these steps:

1. Use the arrow keys to move to the first cell in the range.

2. Press and hold down the Shift key.

3. Use any of the arrow or movement keys to highlight the range. (For more information on the movement keys, see Chapter 9, "Moving Around the Worksheet.") The range appears highlighted on-screen.

Selection Shortcuts

In many cases, you will want to select more than a few cells. You may want to select an entire row or column, or perhaps even the entire worksheet. Excel provides shortcuts for selecting these sections:

To Select	Do This
A column	Click on the column letter or press Ctrl+Spacebar.

To Select	Do This
A row	Click on the row number or press Shift+Spacebar.
An entire worksheet	Click on the Select All button (the blank square above the row numbers and to the left of the column letters) or press Ctrl+Shift+Spacebar.

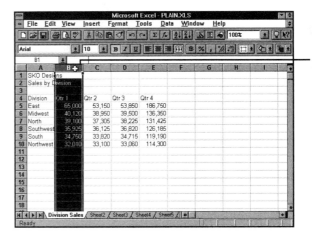

Click on the column letter to select a column.

Click on the row number to select a row.

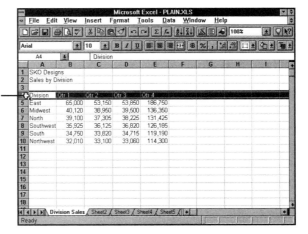

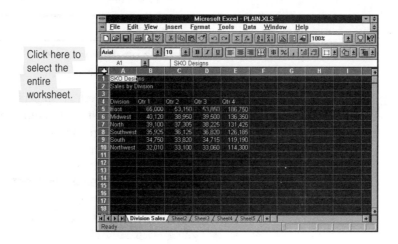

Click here to select the entire worksheet.

Beyond Survival

Selecting a Noncontiguous Range

Press Ctrl and drag To selecT mulTiple ranges

What do you do if the cells you want to select aren't next to each other? Suppose that you want to select some cells in column A and some in column E. In Excel, you aren't limited to selecting cells next to each other. You can select noncontiguous cells by following these steps:

1. Select the first range using any of the methods described earlier in the chapter.

2. Hold down the Ctrl key and select the next range.

3. Repeat step 2 for each additional range you want to select.

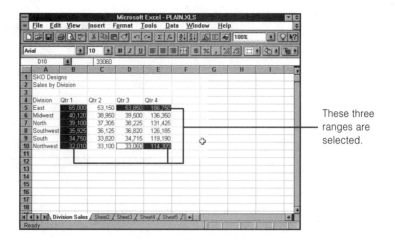

These three ranges are selected.

Moving Within a Selection

When you have a range selected and want to move around within the selected range, you cannot press an arrow key—doing so deselects the range. Instead, use one of the following key combinations to move within a selected area:

Press	To move the active cell
Tab	One cell to the right.
Shift+Tab	One cell to the left.
Enter	Down one cell.
Shift+Enter	Up one cell.
Ctrl+. (period)	Next corner of the selection.

Cheat Sheet

Understanding Formulas

A formula is made up of three parts:

- An equal sign
- Cell references
- The operator

Entering a Formula

1. Select the cell to contain the formula.
2. Type an equal sign.
3. Click on the first cell you want to include.
4. Type an operator.
5. Click on the next cell you want.
6. Repeat steps 4 and 5 until the formula is complete.
7. Press Enter.

Controlling Calculation Manually

1. Select Tools Options.
2. Click the Calculation tab.
3. Click the Manual option button.
4. Click OK.

Manually Recalculating the Worksheet

1. Select Tools Options.
2. Click the Calculation tab.
3. Click the Calc Now button.

12

Entering Formulas

The main reason you spend time entering numbers in a worksheet is so you can perform some calculation on the numbers; you add them, subtract them, multiply them, and so on. To perform calculations, you create a formula—that is, you type the equation.

Basic Survival

Understanding Formulas

When you create a formula, you could type the exact values you want to work with (for instance, 600+1200). But that makes Excel nothing more than an expensive calculator. What makes Excel powerful is its capability to reference a value in a cell. Instead of typing the exact value, you just click on the cell that contains the value you want. Excel uses that value in the current calculation and includes the cell reference in the formula. Then if you change the value in the referenced cell, Excel updates the formula.

Here's an example of a simple formula:

=A1+A2

This formula takes the value in cell A1 and adds it to A2.

Notice that the formula is made up of these parts:

An equal sign (=). The equal sign is what tells Excel that the entry is a formula as opposed to a text or number entry.

Cell references (A1 and A2). You can enter cell references in a formula by clicking on them with the mouse or by typing them.

The operator (+). Here are the most common types of operators:

Operator	Description
+	Addition
–	Subtraction or negation
*	Multiplication
/	Division
%	Percentage
^	Exponentiation
=	Equal
<	Less than
<=	Less than or equal to
>	Greater than
>=	Greater than or equal to
<>	Not equal to

Entering a Formula

To create a formula, you just put together the various pieces—the equal sign, the cell references, and the operators—in the order you want. Follow these steps:

1. Select the cell that will contain the formula.

2. Type an equal sign.

3. Click on the first cell you want to include in the formula. Notice that Excel displays a moving marquee as you move to the selected cell. Or, type in the cell reference instead of clicking on the cell. The cell reference appears in the active cell and in the formula bar. If you want to include a value (for example, 10), simply type that value.

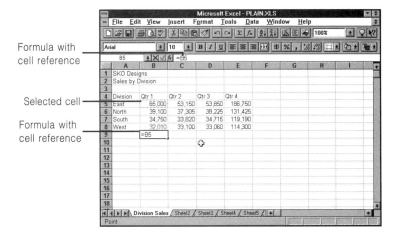

Formula with cell reference

Selected cell

Formula with cell reference

4. Type an operator (from the list above). When you type an operator, Excel moves back to the cell that contains the formula.

5. Click on the next cell you want.

6. Continue typing operators and selecting cells until the formula is complete.

7. When the formula is complete, press Enter. In the formula bar, you see the actual formula. In the cell, you see the results of the formula.

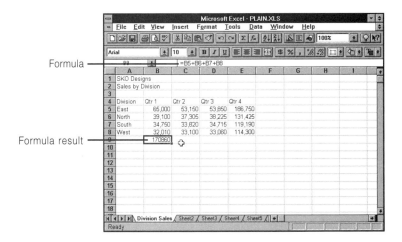

Formula

Formula result

If you get an error message while trying to enter a formula, read the message for information about what is not correct. Then click OK and make the change.

Beyond Survival

Creating Complex Formulas

In some formulas, you may want to perform two calculations. For instance, you may want to add two values and then multiply them by the third. To ensure that Excel performs the calculation in the order you want (adds and then multiplies), you need to be aware of the calculation order. Here's the order Excel uses when calculating a formula:

–	Negation
%	Percentage
^	Exponentiation
* and /	Multiplication and Division
+ and –	Addition and Subtraction

If you want to perform multiple operations within the same formula, you may need to adjust the order of calculations. For example, the formula 5*4+3 can be calculated one of two ways:

Formula	Result
(5*4)+3	23
5*(4+3)	35

Operation in parentheses is done first

To control the order of calculation, use parentheses to surround the part of the equation you want to calculate first.

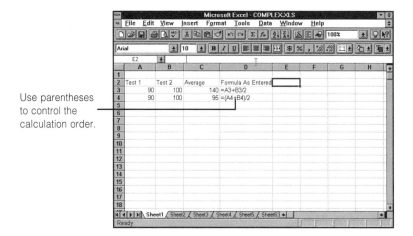

Use parentheses to control the calculation order.

Understanding Cell References

Another concept you need to be familiar with when you create a formula is cell referencing. When you enter a cell reference in a formula, Excel notes the relative relationship of that cell to the cell that contains the formula. For instance, if you sum the two cells above a formula cell, Excel thinks of this as "Go up two cells, take that value and add it to the cell one up." This concept is known as *relative addressing*.

This type of referencing makes it easy to copy and move formulas. Suppose that you want to create a similar formula in the next column. Rather than retype the formula, you can copy it. Since the formula doesn't refer to specific cells (it refers to cells by their relative location), the same formula will work in the next column over. Excel simply adjusts the cell references. Relative addressing enables you to copy and move cells and have the references adjust according to location.

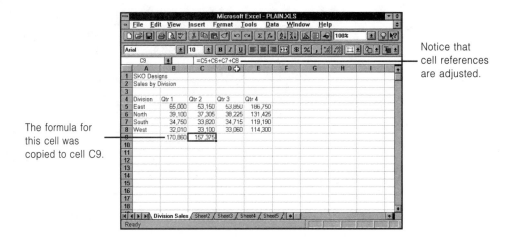

Notice that cell references are adjusted.

The formula for this cell was copied to cell C9.

In some formulas, you may want to refer to a specific cell; you don't want the formula to adjust. In this case, you use a different type of cell reference: a mixed reference or an absolute reference. In a *mixed reference*, you can tell Excel to adjust the column but keep the row reference the same, or to adjust the row but keep the column reference the same. With an *absolute reference*, you tell Excel, "Use this cell—no matter what."

For example, suppose you have a discount rate in cell A2 that you want to use in formulas in column C. Instead of using a relative reference, use an absolute reference.

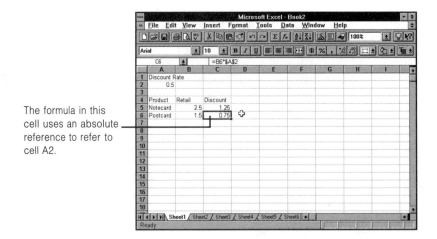

The formula in this cell uses an absolute reference to refer to cell A2.

To change a reference or part of a reference from relative to absolute, type a $ sign before the part you want to make absolute. Here are some examples:

$A1   Always refers to row A, but the column will vary.

A$1   Always refers to column 1, but the row will vary.

A1   Always refers to cell A1.

Controlling Calculation Manually

Because the formula references cells rather than exact values, you can change the value in a cell, and the formula will be recalculated automatically. This flexibility enables you to make changes to key values and see how those changes affect other formulas and cells in the worksheet. For example, what if you increased sales by 15%? What if you budget $25,000 for an item? Make any changes you want, and Excel will recalculate the formulas.

For the most part, automatic calculation works pretty quickly. Excel calculates only those formulas that are affected by edits (as opposed to recalculating all formulas). You can still enter data as Excel is calculating; the calculation will be paused until you finish.

If you'd prefer, you can switch to manual calculation so Excel will calculate the worksheet only when you tell it to. You may want to use manual calculation in particularly large worksheets, where recalculating may take some time.

To change the calculation method, follow these steps:

1. Select the Tools Options command.

2. Click on the Calculation tab. You will see the Calculation tab of the Options dialog box.

3. In the Calculation area, click on the Manual option button.

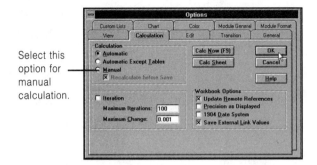

Select this
option for
manual
calculation.

4. Click OK.

___

Manually Recalculating the Worksheet

When you have turned on manual calculation and you make a change to a cell referenced in a formula, Excel displays the word **Calculate** in the status bar as a reminder to recalculate. To recalculate the worksheet, follow these steps:

1. Select the Tools Options command.

2. Click on the Calculation tab.

Press F9 To Calculate Now

3. Click on the Calc Now button. Excel calculates all worksheets.

If you only want to calculate part of a formula, select the part you want to calculate in the formula bar and press F9.

Cheat Sheet

Using AutoSum

1. Select the cell to contain the sum formula.
2. Click the AutoSum button.
3. Make sure the correct range is selected.
4. Press Enter.

Understanding the Parts of a Function

- The function starts with an equal sign.
- Next is the function name.
- Next is a set of parentheses.
- Inside the parentheses are the arguments.

Using the Function Wizard

1. Select the cell to contain the function.
2. Click the Function Wizard button f_x .
3. Click the function category you want.
4. Click the function you want.
5. Click the Next button.
6. Enter values for each argument.
7. Click the Finish button.

Typing a Function

1. Select the cell to contain the function.
2. Type the equal sign.
3. Type the function name and an opening parenthesis.
4. Select the arguments.
5. Type the closing parenthesis.
6. Press Enter.

13

Entering Functions

With Excel, you don't have to be a mathematician to create and use complex formulas. Instead, you can use predefined formulas, called *functions*. Functions provide a shorthand way of entering complex formulas. For example, one of the simplest functions, SUM, condenses a longer formula into a shortened version. Rather than have this formula:

=A1+A2+A3+A4+A5

You can use this function:

=SUM(A1:A5)

Functions also enable you to perform complex calculations, such as figuring a loan amount or determining your rate of return on an investment.

Excel provides a shortcut for creating SUM functions. You can enter other functions by typing them directly or by using the Function Wizard.

Basic Survival

Using AutoSum

The most common calculation used in worksheets is summing a group of numbers. For your convenience, Excel includes an AutoSum button that automatically creates a SUM function, using a best-guess for the range you want to sum.

Here's how Excel figures which range to use. Excel first suggests the range above the selected cell, if those cells contain values. If the cells above the formula cell do not contain values, Excel looks to the left and suggests the range to the left of the selected cell. If no cells above or to the left of the selected cell contain values, Excel enters **=SUM( )**.

Follow these steps to use AutoSum:

1. Select the cell that you want to contain the sum formula.

2. Click the AutoSum button. Excel guesses which cells you want to sum and surrounds them with a marquee.

Selected
SUM range

SUM formula

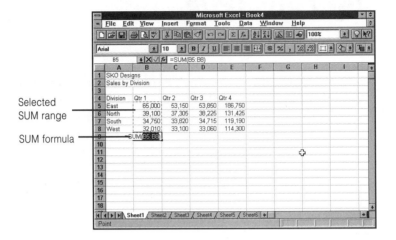

3. Make sure that the correct range is selected. If that range is correct, go on to step 4. If it is not correct, select the range you want to sum.

4. Press Enter. Excel enters the function into the cell. In the cell, you see the results of the function. When the cell is selected, you see the actual function in the formula bar.

ATT + = for
SUM formula

Function

Result of
function

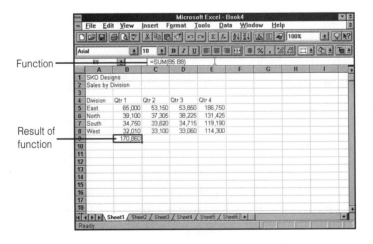

Understanding the Parts of a Function

Notice in the SUM function that, like a formula, the function is made up of different parts. Like a formula, the function starts with an equal sign. The next part is the function name, usually a short, abbreviated word that indicates what the function does. After the function name is a set of parentheses, which contain the *arguments*—the values used in the calculation. Different functions require different arguments. For the function to work properly, you must enter the parts in the correct order and format. For information on the most commonly used functions, see Appendix B, "A Function Directory."

Using the Function Wizard

Manually putting together the parts of a function can be difficult— especially if you don't know which arguments you need to enter. To help you build a function, you can use Excel's Function Wizard. This wizard leads you step by step through the process of entering the different parts of a function.

To use the Function Wizard, follow these steps:

1. Select the cell you want to contain the function.

2. Select the Insert Function command or click the Function Wizard button f_*. The Function Wizard - Step 1 of 2 dialog box appears. It lists the most recently used functions in the Function Name list. Other categories are listed in the Function Category list.

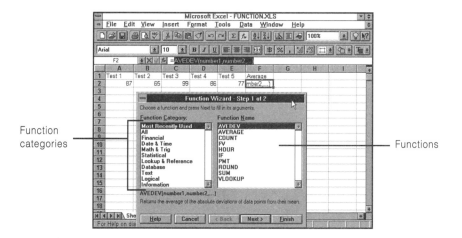

Function categories

Functions

3. In the Function Category list, click on the function category you want. The Function Name list changes, showing the functions in the selected category.

4. In the Function Name list, click on the function you want. Notice that Excel lists the function format and a short description at the bottom of the dialog box.

Click Help button for more info

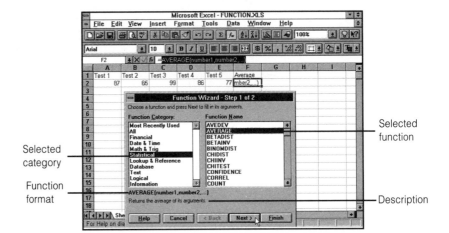

5. Click on the Next button. Excel displays the Function Wizard - Step 2 of 2 dialog box. Here you enter the arguments for the function. Basically, arguments can be a single value, a single cell reference, a series of cell references or values, or a range. Some arguments are mandatory—they appear in boldface in the dialog box. Others are optional—they are not boldface.

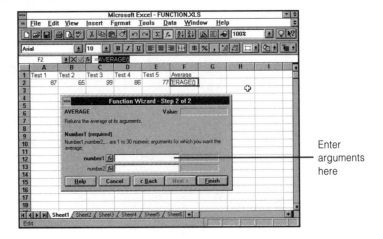

6. Enter values for each of the arguments. You can click on a cell in the worksheet or drag across a range. You can also type the cell reference or range reference directly in the argument text box, or you can type a value in the Value text box.

7. Press Enter or click on the Finish button. Excel creates the function.

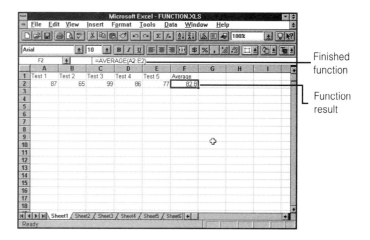

Finished function

Function result

Beyond Survival

Typing a Function

If you know the appropriate format for the function, you can type it directly into the worksheet cell—just as if you were creating a formula. Follow these steps:

1. Select the cell you want to contain the function.

2. Type the equal sign.

3. Type the function name and an opening parenthesis.

4. Type, click on, or select the arguments for the function.

5. Type the closing parenthesis.

6. Press Enter.

The following figure shows examples of different functions and their results.

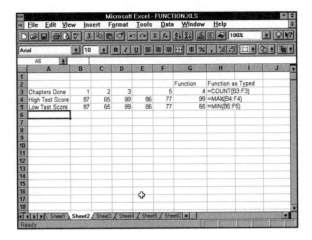

If you get an error message while trying to enter a function, click on
the Help button. You will get instant help on the function you are
using. Read the information and then make any necessary changes to
the function.

Cheat Sheet

In-Cell Editing

1. Double-click the cell you want to edit.
2. Click the place where you want the cursor.
3. Make any changes.
4. Press Enter.

Editing in the Formula Bar

1. Select the cell to edit.
2. Click in the formula bar or press F2.
3. Click the place where you want the cursor.
4. Make any changes.
5. Press Enter.

Editing Tips

- Click the Cancel box to cancel the change.
- Click the Confirm box to accept the change.
- Click the Name box to insert a range name.
- Click the Function Wizard box to start the Function Wizard.

14

Editing Data

If you make a mistake when creating a worksheet, you can easily edit the entry. The fact that you can make changes to the values in your worksheet is what makes Excel such a valuable analysis tool. You can change a key value and see how it affects the bottom line. You can edit the entry directly in the cell or in the formula bar.

Basic Survival

In-Cell Editing

In previous versions of Excel, you had to edit the entry in the formula bar. With Excel 5, you can edit the entry right in the cell. Follow these steps to edit a cell:

1. Select the cell you want to edit.

2. Double-click the mouse button or press F2. The insertion point appears within the current cell.

Insertion point →

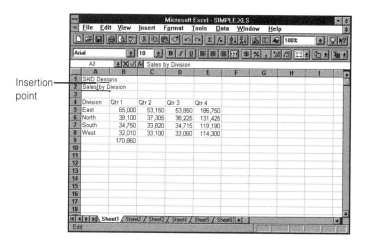

3. Move the mouse and click on the position in which you want to make the change. You can also use the arrow keys if you want.

4. Make any changes. See the upcoming section called "Editing Tips" for information about shortcuts you can use when editing a cell.

5. Press Enter. Excel updates the entry.

Arrow keys
DO NOT
move To
anoTher cell

When editing a cell, you cannot press an arrow key to confirm the entry and move to another cell. Arrow keys move the cursor within the cell, but do not move the cell selector. You must press Enter to move to a different cell.

Beyond Survival

Editing in the Formula Bar

If you prefer, you can make changes in the formula bar instead of in the cell. Follow these steps:

1. Select the cell you want to edit.

2. Click within the formula bar. The insertion point appears in the formula bar.

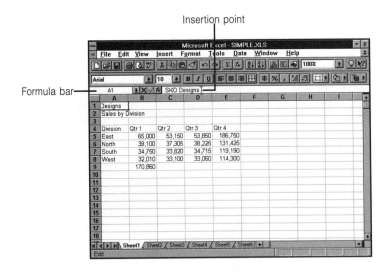

Insertion point

Formula bar

3. Move the mouse and click on the position in which you want to make the change. You can also use the arrow keys if you want.

4. Make any changes. See the upcoming section called "Editing Tips" for information about shortcuts you can use when editing a cell.

5. Press Enter. Excel updates the entry.

Editing Tips

To move the insertion point to the spot you want, you can use the following keys:

Press	To
→	Move right one character.
←	Move left one character.
Home	Move to the beginning of the line or cell.
End	Move to the end of the line or cell.
Ctrl+→	Move right one word.
Ctrl+←	Move left one word.
Backspace	Delete the character to the left of the insertion point.
Delete	Delete the character to the right of the insertion point.
Ctrl+Del	Delete from the insertion point to the end of the line or cell.

You can also drag across characters to select them. If you want to delete the selected characters, just press Delete.

In addition, as you edit, the formula bar displays buttons next to the entry. You can use these buttons to insert functions or range names, or to confirm or cancel the entry.

- Click the Cancel box to cancel the change.

- Click the Confirm box to confirm the change.

- Click the Name box to insert a range name in the entry. See Chapter 39, "Using Names" for more information on range names.

- Click the Function Wizard button to start the Function Wizard. See Chapter 13, "Entering Functions," for more information on functions and the Function Wizard.

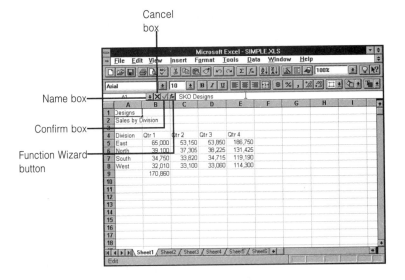

Cheat Sheet

Deleting Cell Contents

1. Select the cell or range to delete.
2. Press Delete.

Undoing a Deletion

- Select Edit Undo.

  OR

- Click the Undo button .

15

Deleting Data

As you create your worksheet, you may find that you need to delete some entries. Perhaps they aren't valid anymore, or perhaps you entered something incorrectly. It's not a problem with Excel, because you can easily delete cell contents.

Basic Survival

Deleting Cell Contents

If an entry is no longer valid, you can delete it. Keep in mind that when you delete cell contents, any formulas that reference this cell are updated. Follow these steps:

1. Select the cell or range you want to delete.

Range you want to delete ─────

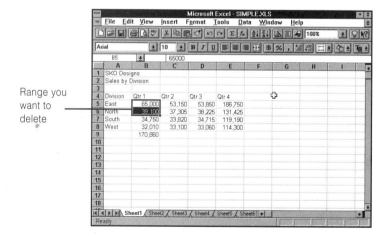

2. Press Delete.

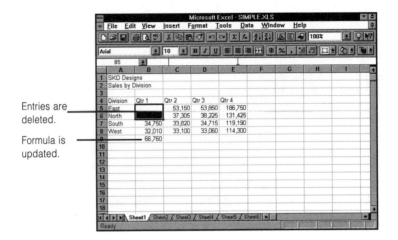

Entries are deleted.

Formula is updated.

Beyond Survival

Undoing a Deletion

If you delete a selected cell or range by accident, immediately select the Edit Undo command or click on the Undo button. If you do this immediately, you can undo the deletion. If you have performed some other task since you deleted an entry, you cannot undo the deletion. Excel can undo only the last action performed.

For information on deleting cell formatting (not cell contents), see Chapter 22, "Formatting Data." To delete both the cell contents and the cells themselves, see Chapter 36, "Deleting Cells, Rows, and Columns."

Cheat Sheet

Moving Data with the Command Method

1. Select the cell or range to move.
2. Click the Cut button ✂ .
3. Select the cell at the upper left corner of where you want the cells pasted.
4. Click the Paste button 📋 .

Moving Data with the Drag-and-Drop Method

1. Select the cell or range to move.
2. Point to the selection's border.
3. Drag the border.
4. Release the mouse button.

Inserting Cut Cells

1. Select the cell or range to move.
2. Click the Cut button ✂ .
3. Select the cell at the upper left corner of where you want the pasted cells inserted.
4. Select Insert Cut Cells.

16

Moving Data

In order to get all your data in the right spot, you should spend some time planning your worksheets before you create them (see Chapter 8, "Planning Your Worksheet"). However, if you don't get it right the first time, you can easily rearrange the worksheet. Rather than starting over and retyping everything, you can just move things around.

Basic Survival

Moving Data with the Command Method

When you want to move selected data farther than the current screen, consider using the command method. If you are just learning Excel, the command method is probably best for you. The other method, the drag-and-drop method that is covered in the next section, takes some practice getting used to.

To move data using commands, follow these steps:

1. Select the cell or range you want to move.

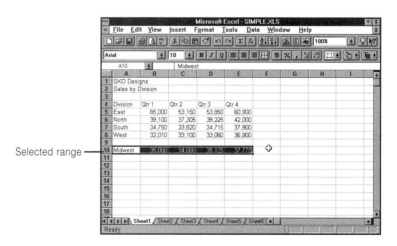

Selected range

2. Select the Edit Cut command or click on the Cut button ✂ .
Excel displays a moving marquee around the selected cells and
prompts you to select a destination.

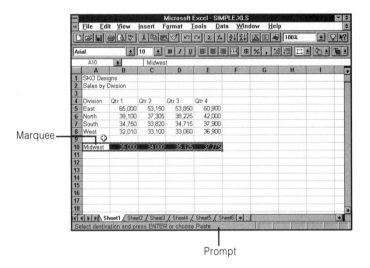

Marquee

Prompt

3. Select the cell at the upper left corner of where you want the
pasted cells. Keep in mind that Excel will overwrite any cells in the
destination area. Be sure to select a blank area or an area that you
want to overwrite.

4. Press Enter, select the Edit Paste command, or click on the Paste
button 📋 .

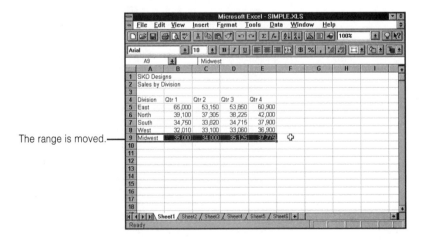

The range is moved.

$Ctrl + X =$
CUT

$Ctrl + V =$
$PasTe$

When you move cells that are referenced in a formula, all relative references are adjusted to reflect the new location. All absolute references remain the same. See Chapter 12, "Entering Formulas," for more information on cell references.

Beyond Survival

Moving Data with the Drag-and-Drop Method

If you want to move a selected range a short distance, use the drag-and-drop method. This method takes some practice because you have to get the mouse pointer in just the right spot. If you put it in the wrong spot, you may deselect the range or fill the range. Because it takes some practice, you may want to wait until you become more comfortable with the program before you use this method.

To move data using the drag-and-drop method, follow these steps:

1. Select the cell or range you want moved.

2. Move the mouse pointer over the selection's border. The mouse pointer should change to an arrow.

3. Drag the border. As you drag, you see an outline of the selected data.

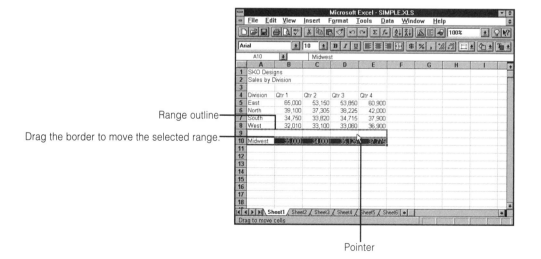

Range outline —

Drag the border to move the selected range.

Pointer

4. When the data is in the spot you want, release the mouse button.

Be sure to drag to a blank area of the worksheet. If you drag to a location that contains entries, you'll overwrite those entries.

If drag-and-drop doesn't work, make sure that the feature is turned on. The feature is located in the Options dialog box, which you access by selecting the Tools Options command. In the Options dialog box, click on the Edit tab, and then check the Allow Cell Drag-and-Drop option. Click OK.

Inserting Cut Cells

If you want to move a range within an area that already contains data, you can have Excel insert the cut cells within the existing entries without overwriting those entries. In actuality, Excel inserts new cells first, and then pastes the data into those new cells. Follow these steps:

1. Select the cell or range you want to move.

2. Select the Edit Cut command or click on the Cut button ✂ . Excel displays a moving marquee around the selected cells and prompts you to select a destination.

3. Select the cell at the upper left corner of where you want the pasted cells inserted. Excel will push existing cells down or to the right to insert the new data.

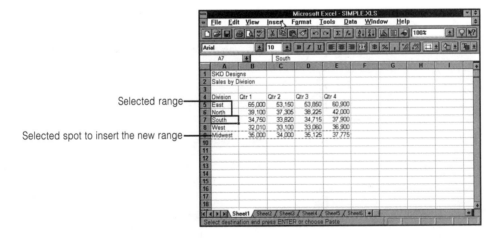

Selected range

Selected spot to insert the new range

4. Select the Insert Cut Cells command. Excel makes room for the selected range and inserts the cut cells into the existing area.

The selected range is inserted here.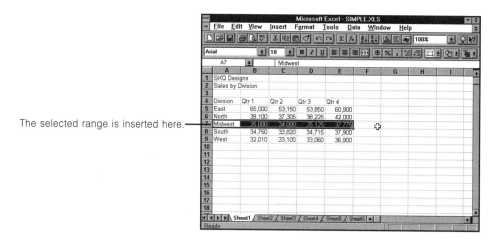

Cheat Sheet

Copying Data with the Command Method

1. Select the cell or range to copy.
2. Click the Copy button 📋.
3. Select the cell at the upper left corner of where you want the pasted cells.
4. Click the Paste button 📋.

Copying Data with the Drag-and-Drop Method

1. Select the cell or range to copy.
2. Point at one of the selection's borders.
3. Hold down Ctrl.
4. Drag the copy of the selection to a new location.
5. Release Ctrl and the mouse button.

Copying and Inserting

1. Select the cell or range to copy.
2. Click the Copy button 📋.
3. Select the cell at the upper left of where you want the pasted cells inserted.
4. Select Insert Copied Cells.
5. Click OK.

Pasting Values Instead of Formulas

1. Select the range to copy.
2. Click the Copy button 📋.
3. Select the range where you want to paste the copy.
4. Select Edit Paste Special.
5. Click the Values option button.
6. Click OK.

17

Copying Data

Entering data in a worksheet would be pretty cumbersome if you had to type each formula or entry. Instead, you can copy formulas or entries to make data entry quick and easy.

Note that when you copy *values*, you make an exact copy of the values. On the other hand, Excel treats formulas a little differently. When you copy a *formula*, all relative references are adjusted to reflect the new location. For instance, if you have the formula =SUM(B1:B5) in B6 and copy the formula to C6, the formula adjusts to =SUM(C1:C5).

Unlike relative references, all absolute references remain the same. For more information on cell references and formulas, see Chapter 12, "Entering Formulas." Another feature that is useful for quick data entry is the fill feature. See Chapter 18, "Filling Data," for information on this feature.

Basic Survival

Copying Data with the Command Method

When you are first learning to use Excel, you will probably want to use the command method to copy. Copying with the drag-and-drop method, described in the next section, takes some practice. Follow these steps to copy data:

1. Select the cell or range you want to copy.

2. Select the Edit Copy command or click on the Copy button 📋. Excel displays a marquee around the selected cell or range.

Formula you want to copy —

Marquee —

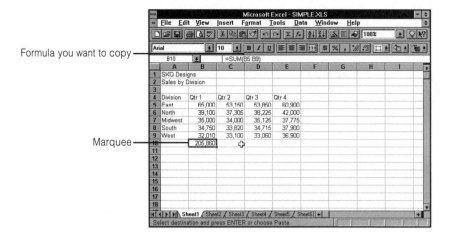

3. **Select the cell at the upper left corner** of where you want the pasted cells if you are pasting a range. If you want to paste a single cell across a range, select the range. Excel pastes data in a range in the same amount of rows and columns as the original. Be careful not to overwrite existing data.

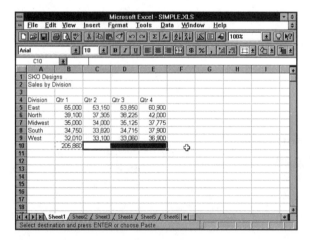

4. **Press Enter, select the Edit Paste command**, or click on the Paste button ![Paste button]. Excel pastes the copy or copies.

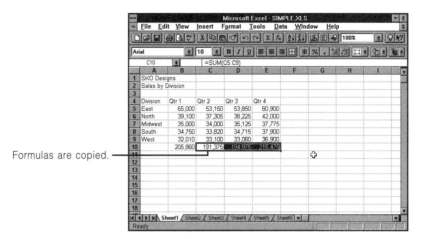

Formulas are copied.

$CTrl + C =$
$Copy$
$CTrl + V =$
$PaSTe$

Note that if you select a range before choosing Edit Copy, and the range is smaller and a different shape than the original, you'll see a message that says the copy and paste areas are different shapes. Click OK, and then either select a range the same size and shape or select only the upper left corner for the pasted range.

Beyond Survival

Copying Data with the Drag-and-Drop Method

If you want to copy a selection to a location that is a short distance away, you can use the drag-and-drop method. Because it takes some practice, you may want to wait until you become more comfortable with the program before you use this method.

Follow these steps to copy data using drag-and-drop:

1. Select the cell or range you want to copy.

2. Put the mouse pointer on a border. The pointer should look like an arrow.

3. Press and hold down the Ctrl key and the mouse button.

4. Drag the copy to a new location. As you drag, note that the mouse pointer includes a plus sign. This indicates that you are copying, rather than moving, the selected range.

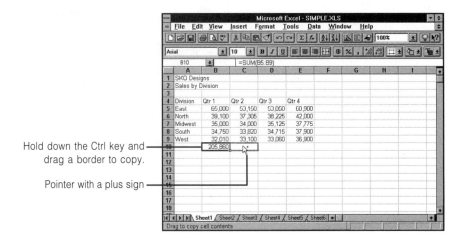

Hold down the Ctrl key and drag a border to copy.

Pointer with a plus sign

5. Release the Ctrl key and mouse button. Excel makes a copy.

Copying and Inserting

If you want to put a copy of selected cells within an area that already contains data, you can have Excel insert the copied cells within the existing entries without overwriting them. (Excel actually inserts new cells first, and then pastes the data into those new cells.) Follow these steps to insert cells that have been copied to the Clipboard:

1. Select the cell or range you want to copy.

2. Select the Edit Copy command or click on the Copy button 📋. Excel displays a moving marquee around the selected cells. You are prompted to select a destination.

3. Select the cell at the upper left corner of where you want the pasted cells inserted. Excel will push existing cells down or to the right to insert the new data.

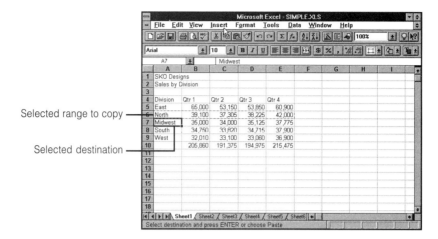

Selected range to copy

Selected destination

4. Select the Insert Copied Cells command. Excel displays the Insert Paste dialog box.

5. Click OK. Excel makes room for the data and inserts the cells into the existing area.

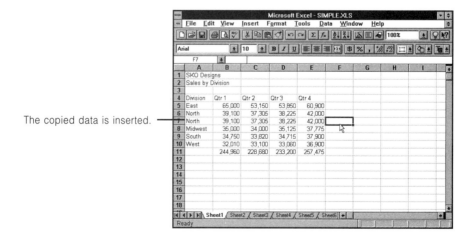

The copied data is inserted.

111

Transposing Data

Transposing (flipping rows and columns) is a special copy operation you might need to use. Suppose that your worksheet is set up with quarters in rows and divisions in columns, but your business analyst prefers the quarters in columns and divisions in rows. Do you have to re-enter all the data? No, you can just transpose it by following these steps:

1. Select the range you want to transpose.

2. Click on the Copy button 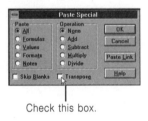. Excel displays a marquee around the selected range and prompts you for the destination.

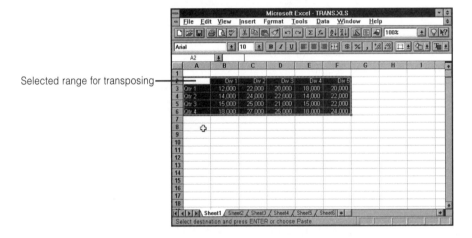

Selected range for transposing

3. Select the first cell where you want to paste the range.

4. Select the Edit Paste Special command. You see the Paste Special dialog box.

5. Click the Transpose check box.

Check this box.

6. Click OK.

Original range

Transposed range

Pasting Values Instead of Formulas

In most cases, you will want formulas to calculate certain values in a worksheet, and you will want these values updated each time you make a change. However, in some cases, you may want just the results of the formula. For example, suppose that you are considering raising prices by 10%, so you create a formula to calculate the new prices. The price raise is approved, and now you want to use the actual value (not the formula) in the cell. In this case, you can copy the formulas, and then paste them back in the same location as values. That way, the values won't change as you change worksheet data (as they would if they were copied as formulas).

To paste values, follow these steps:

1. Select the range you want to copy.

2. Click on the Copy button 🖺. Excel displays a marquee around the selected cells.

3. Select the range where you want to paste the copy. If you want to paste over the original range, select that range.

4. Select the Edit Paste Special command. You see the Paste Special dialog box.

Formulas you want
to paste as values.

Select this option
to paste values.

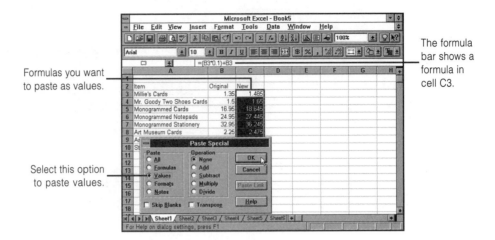

The formula
bar shows a
formula in
cell C3.

5. Click on the Values option button.

6. Click OK. Excel pastes the values over the formulas.

Values rather
than formulas

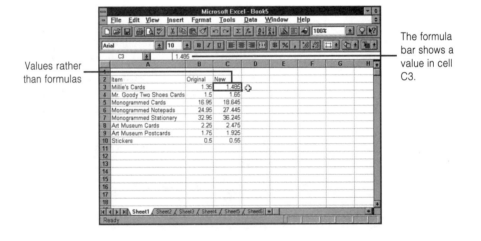

The formula
bar shows a
value in cell
C3.

Cheat Sheet

Understanding How a Fill Works

- To fill the same information, enter the value you want to fill in the first cell of the range.
- To fill a series of numbers, enter the first two numbers in the first two cells of the range.
- To fill dates, enter the first date.

Filling with the Fill Handle

1. Type the entry into the first cell.
2. Select the range that contains the entry.
3. Hold down the mouse button on the fill handle.
4. Drag across the range you want to fill.
5. Release the mouse button.

Filling a Series

1. Type the first entry into the cell.
2. Select the range you want to fill.
3. Select Edit Fill Series.
4. Select to fill rows or columns.
5. Select the type of fill.
6. If you select date as the type of fill, select a date unit.
7. Enter a step value.
8. Enter a stop value.
9. Click OK.

18

Filling Data

Suppose that you want to use a series of months as column heads. Do you have to type each month individually? Not with Excel. You can enter the first month and *fill* the remaining months across a selected range. You can also use this timesaving technique to fill in a series of numbers, text entries, dates, and formulas.

Basic Survival

Understanding How a Fill Works

You can fill a range with a series of numbers, text, dates, and formulas. Depending on what you enter in the first cell or first two cells, Excel will fill the range with what it thinks is the rest of the series. You can use this feature to produce any of the following results:

To fill a series of numbers, enter the first two numbers

- If you want to copy the same information from one cell to others across a range, enter the value you want to copy in the first cell in that range. When you fill, Excel will fill all the cells in the selected range with the same entry.

- If you want to enter a series of numbers, enter the first two numbers of the series in two adjacent cells. For example, to enter a series of numbers in increments of 10, you would enter 10 and 20 in two neighboring cells. When you tell Excel to fill the next two cells, the numbers 30 and 40 appear in them.

- To fill dates, enter the first date, and Excel will increment the date by one. If you want to increment by a different value, enter the first two dates into adjacent cells, and then fill the dates.

- If you are filling a text entry and it contains a number, Excel will increment the number in the fill. For instance, if you enter Qtr 1 and then fill a range, Excel will enter Qtr 2, Qtr 3, and so on.

- If you enter a formula and then fill the entry across a range, Excel copies the formula. Any relative references are adjusted; absolute references remain the same. See Chapter 12, "Entering Formulas" for more information on cell references.

117

The following figure provides some examples of each of these fill types. You can also create a custom fill, for instance, creating a list of parts or clients. For information on this type of fill, see Chapter 38, "Creating a Custom List."

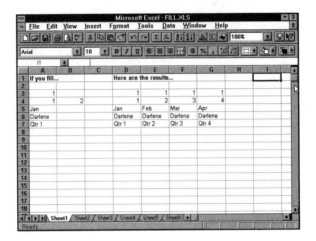

Filling with the Fill Handle

The easiest way to fill a range is to use the fill handle. You can fill as large a range as you want. To do so, follow these steps:

1. **Type the entry into the first cell.** If you want to use a series, enter the first two values in two adjoining cells.

2. **Select the cell or cells that contain the entry.**

3. **Click and hold down the mouse button on the fill handle** in the lower right corner of the cell. The pointer appears as a small cross.

Fill handle ——

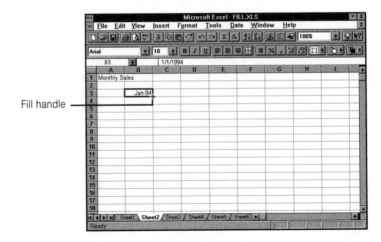

4. Drag across the range you want to fill. As you drag, you will see an outline.

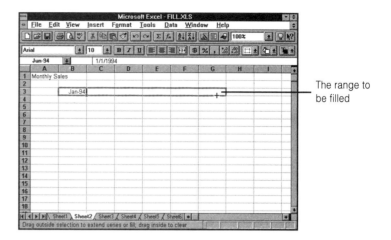

The range to be filled

5. Release the mouse button, and Excel fills the selected cells.

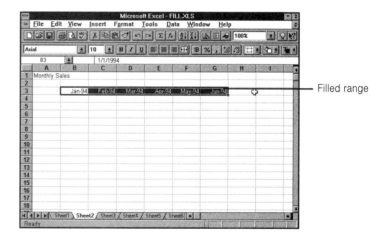

Filled range

Beyond Survival

Filling a Series

If you want to create a different type of fill or a more complex fill, you can use the Fill Series command. For example, you may want to fill a range of weekdays or months. Follow these steps to use the Fill Series command:

1. Type the first entry into the first cell in the range you want to fill.

119

2. Select the range you want to fill.

3. Select the Edit Fill Series command. You see the Series dialog box.

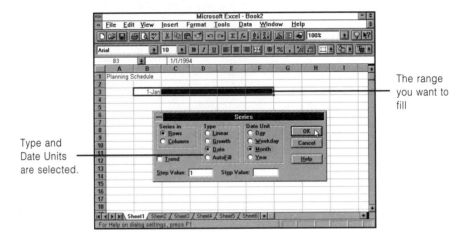

The range you want to fill

Type and
Date Units
are selected.

4. Click in Rows or Columns to tell Excel how to fill the series. If you selected a range in step 2, Excel selects the appropriate option.

5. Select the Type of fill you want to create: Linear, Growth, Date, or AutoFill.

6. If you selected Date for step 5, select a Date Unit: Day, Weekday, Month, or Year.

7. Type a step value in the Step Value text box. The default is 1.

8. Type a stop value in the Stop Value text box, if necessary.

9. Click OK. Excel fills the range.

The range is
filled.

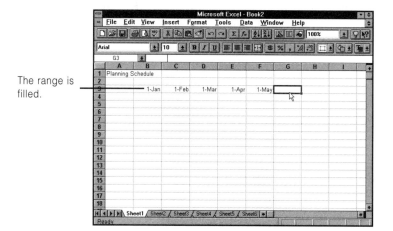

Cheat Sheet

Scrolling Through the Worksheet

- Click on a sheet tab to go to a new worksheet.
- Use the scroll bars to go to a sheet tab that is not visible.

Naming a Sheet

1. Double-click on the sheet tab.
2. Type a name.
3. Click OK.

Inserting a Sheet

1. Select where you want to insert the new worksheet.
2. Select Insert Worksheet.

Deleting a Sheet

1. Select the sheet you want to delete.
2. Select Edit Delete Sheet.
3. Click OK.

Selecting a Group of Sheets

- To select contiguous sheets, hold down Shift and click on the last sheet.
- To select noncontiguous sheets, hold down Ctrl while you click on the sheets.
- To select all sheets, display the shortcut menu and click on Select All Sheets.

Moving or Copying a Sheet

1. Click the sheet tab.
2. To move, drag the tab to a new location. To copy, hold down Ctrl while dragging.
3. Release the mouse button.

19

Working with Worksheets

When you start Excel, you don't have just one worksheet available. You have a set of worksheets, like a pad of worksheet paper. For simple worksheets, you may just use the first sheet. For more complex worksheets, you might need to use several sheets. For instance, you can enter sales results on one sheet for division 1 sales, sales results on another sheet for division 2 sales, and so on.

A set of worksheets is called a *workbook*. When you save the workbook, all sheets are saved together in the workbook. For more information on saving, see Chapter 20, "Saving and Closing a Workbook."

Basic Survival

Scrolling Through the Worksheets

When you start Excel, 16 worksheets are included in the workbook. The sheets are named Sheet1, Sheet2, and so on; the names appear on sheet tabs along the bottom of the workbook window. Sheet1 is the active worksheet.

Selecting a sheet is simple: just click on the sheet tab. If the sheet tab you want is not visible, you can scroll to the other sheets in the workbook. To do so, use the sheet scroll controls at the bottom left corner of the worksheet.

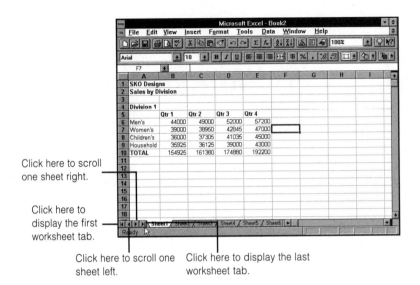

Click here to scroll one sheet right.

Click here to display the first worksheet tab.

Click here to scroll one sheet left.

Click here to display the last worksheet tab.

Naming a Sheet

The default names, Sheet1, Sheet2, and so on, aren't very descriptive. If you use several sheets in a workbook, you should rename them so that you know what each sheet contains. To rename a sheet, follow these steps:

1. Double-click on the sheet tab of the sheet you want to rename. Or, select the sheet tab and then select the Format Sheet Rename command. You see the Rename Sheet dialog box.

Type the new name here.

2. Type a name. You can include spaces in the name and type up to 31 characters.

3. Click OK. Excel displays the new name on the worksheet tab.

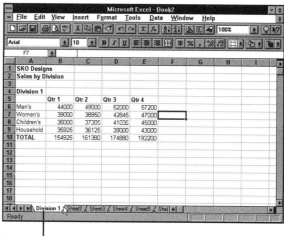

New sheet name

Make sure that you don't confuse *worksheet* names with *workbook* (file) names. They aren't the same. You still need to name and save the workbook separately, as described in the next chapter.

Inserting a Sheet

As mentioned, a workbook by default includes 16 sheets. You can easily add more sheets, if needed. To do so, follow these steps:

1. Select the worksheet where you want to insert the new worksheet. The new worksheet will be inserted *before* this worksheet.

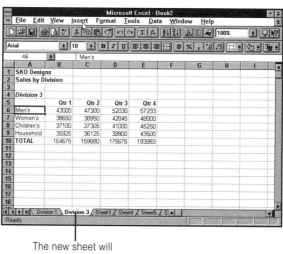

The new sheet will be inserted before this sheet.

2. Select the Insert Worksheet command, and Excel inserts a new sheet.

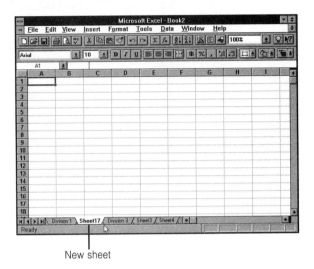

New sheet

RighT-click on The sheeT Tab for shorTcuT menu

If you want, you can use the shortcut menu instead of the menu command. Point to a sheet tab and click the right mouse button, and then click on the command you want.

Deleting a Sheet

If you don't want extra sheets in your workbook, you can delete them. If you do this, Excel will delete not only the sheet, but all the data on that sheet—so be sure you don't delete sheets that contain information you need. Also keep in mind that you can't undo a worksheet insertion or deletion. If you insert a worksheet by mistake, just delete it. If you delete a worksheet by mistake, there's nothing you can do.

ImporTanT!

Follow these steps to delete a sheet:

1. Select the sheet you want to delete. If you want to delete more than one sheet, select them all, as described in the next section.

2. Select the Edit Delete Sheet command.

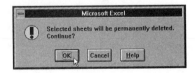

3. Click OK to confirm the deletion. The worksheet and all its data are deleted. Excel does not renumber existing default sheet names.

Beyond Survival

Selecting a Group of Sheets

If you want to work on several sheets at once—perhaps to delete several sheets—you can select more than one. To select more than one sheet, click on the first sheet you want to select. Then do one of the following:

- To select sheets next to each other, press and hold down the **Shift** key and click on the last sheet. All sheets between and including the first and last are selected.

- To select sheets that aren't next to each other, hold down the **Ctrl** key and click on each individual sheet.

- To select all sheets, click the right mouse button on a sheet tab to display the shortcut menu. Click on the **Select All Sheets** command.

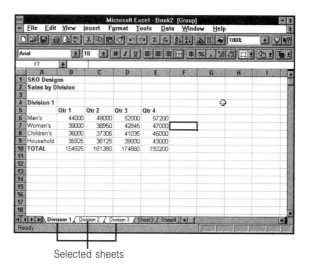

Selected sheets

When several sheets are selected, **[Group]** appears in the workbook title bar next to the file name. To ungroup a selected set of sheets, click on another sheet, or click the right mouse button on a sheet tab and select the Ungroup Sheets command.

Moving a Sheet

If you don't plan the order as you create your sheets, the sheets may appear out of order. For instance, suppose that you have sales from Division 2 on Sheet 1, sales from Division 3 on Sheet 2, sales from Division 1 on Sheet 3, and the summary information on Sheet 4. You can rearrange them in this order:

Summary Sales	Sheet 1
Division 1 Sales	Sheet 2
Division 2 Sales	Sheet 3
Division 3 Sales	Sheet 4

To move a sheet to another location in the workbook, follow these steps:

1. Click on the tab of the sheet you want to move.

2. Drag the tab to the new location. As you drag, you see a document icon.

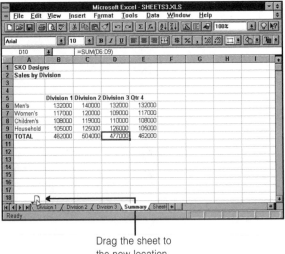

Drag the sheet to
the new location.

3. When the sheet tab is in the position you want, release the mouse button. Excel rearranges the sheets.

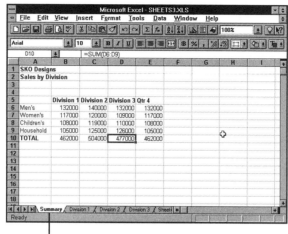

Sheets are rearranged.

You can also move a sheet to another workbook. To do so, click on the sheet tab and select the **Edit Move or Copy Sheet** command. In the Move or Copy dialog box that appears, select the workbook from the To Book drop-down list. Then click OK.

Copying a Sheet

When you copy a sheet in the same workbook, Excel adds a number (2, 3, 4, depending on the number of the copy) to the sheet name. If you don't like the name, you can rename the worksheet.

To copy a sheet within the workbook, follow these steps:

1. Click on the sheet tab.

2. Hold down the Ctrl key and drag the tab to the new location.

You can also copy a sheet to another workbook. To do so, click on the sheet tab and select the Edit Move or Copy Sheet command. In the Move or Copy dialog box that appears, select the workbook from the To Book drop-down list. Check the Create a Copy check box. Then click OK.

Cheat Sheet

Saving and Naming a Worksheet

1. Click the Save button 🖫 .
2. Select a drive and directory.
3. Type a file name in the File Name text box.
4. Click OK.
5. If prompted, enter file summary information and click OK.

Saving a Workbook Again

- Select File Save.

  OR

- Click the Save button 🖫 .

Closing a Workbook

- Select File Close.

  OR

- Double-click the workbook's Control-menu box.

Saving a Workbook with a New Name

1. Select File Save As.
2. Select a drive and directory.
3. Type a file name in the File Name text box.
4. Click OK.
5. If prompted, enter file summary information and click OK.

Saving a Workbook with a Password

1. Select File Save As.
2. Select a drive and directory.
3. Type a file name in the File Name text box.
4. Click the Options button.
5. Enter a password in one of the text boxes.
6. When prompted, retype the password and press Enter.
7. Click OK.

20

Saving and Closing a Workbook

The most important thing you need to remember is to save your workbook. As you type entries into a workbook, the information is stored in RAM (random access memory), which is temporary memory. If the power is turned off for any reason, you'll lose all the information you have entered. To avoid this problem, you need to save the workbook as you work on it.

Basic Survival

Saving and Naming a Workbook

The first time you save the workbook, you are prompted for a file name. You need to name the file so that you can find it and open it again later. To save and name a workbook, follow these steps:

1. Select the File Save command or click on the Save button 🔲. You will see the Save As dialog box.

Type the file name here.
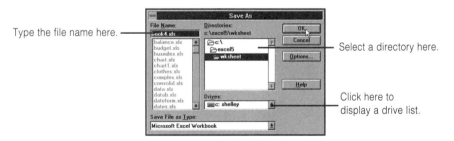
Select a directory here.

Click here to display a drive list.

2. If you want to save the file to another drive, display the Drives drop-down list and select the drive you want.

3. If you want to save the file in another directory, select that directory from the Directories list.

4. Type a file name in the File Name text box. When saving files, use a descriptive name—one that will help you remember the contents of the workbook. You can use up to eight characters in the file name; let Excel assign the file extension (.XLS).

131

5. Click OK.

6. If you are prompted, enter any file summary information and click OK. (See the section "Entering Summary Information" later in this chapter.) Excel displays the name of the workbook in the title bar.

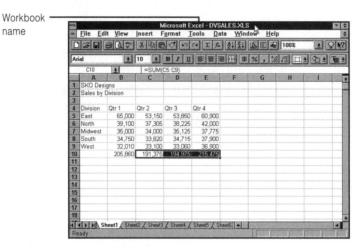

Workbook name

Ctrl + S = Save

Saving a Workbook Again

Keep in mind that you shouldn't save just once. You should continue to save as you work on the workbook. When you save the workbook, the information is written to disk. But as you continue to make changes, those changes aren't reflected in the disk version of the file until you save the file again. It's a good idea to save every five to ten minutes or so.

Remember! Save often!

To save the workbook again, just select the File Save command or click on the Save button 🖫. Excel will save the workbook using the original name.

Closing a Workbook

When you are finished working on a workbook, you should close it. You can have several workbooks on-screen at once, but closing workbooks you no longer need will save memory. To close a workbook, select the File Close command.

When all workbooks are closed, you see only two menu names: File and Help. Using the File menu, you can choose to create a new workbook or open an existing workbook, as described in the next chapter.

Ctrl + F4
To Close

Use this menu to create a new workbook or open an existing workbook.

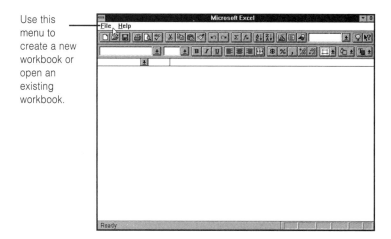

If you have several workbooks open, you can close them all by holding down the Shift key when you click on File in the menu bar. The Close command changes to Close All. Click this command to close all open workbooks. For information on working with more than one workbook, see Chapter 21, "Opening a Workbook."

Beyond Survival

Saving a Workbook with a New Name

If you don't like the original name you assigned to a workbook, you can use the File Save As command to rename the file. This command also comes in handy when you decide to keep the version of the file on disk intact, but save the on-screen version also. For instance, suppose that you create a sales worksheet for one division. You save that on disk as SALEDIV1. You need the same information in a worksheet for division 2. You can open the SALEDIV1 workbook and save it as SALEDIV2. You can then modify SALEDIV2, while leaving SALEDIV1 intact.

In addition, you might want to use File Save As when you want to change something about how the file is saved—for instance, to add a password or change the file type.

Using File Save As is also a good way to make a backup copy of a workbook. You can save the file to a different directory or disk so that you have two copies: the original and the newly saved file.

Follow these steps to save a workbook with a new name:

1. Select the File Save As command. The Save As dialog box appears.

Type the file name here.

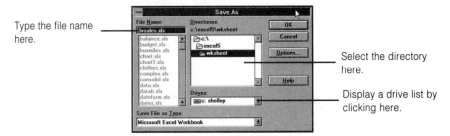

Select the directory here.

Display a drive list by clicking here.

2. If you want to save the file to another drive, display the Drives drop-down list and select the drive you want.

3. If you want to save the file in another directory, select that directory in the Directories list.

4. Type a file name in the File Name text box.

5. Click OK.

6. If you are prompted, enter any file summary information and click OK. See the section "Entering Summary Information" later in this chapter. Excel saves the workbook with the new name.

Saving a Workbook with a Password

If your workbook contains sensitive information, you can assign a password to a workbook so that anyone trying to open or save changes to a file will be prompted to type the password.

To save a workbook with a password, follow these steps:

1. If you are saving the file for the first time, select the File Save command. If you have saved and named the file once and want to add a password, select the File Save As command.

2. Select the appropriate drive and directory.

3. Type a file name in the File Name text box. (If you've already saved the file, you don't need to type the name, unless you want to save the file with a new name.)

4. Click on the Options button. You see the Save Options dialog box.

Type a password here.

5. Enter a password in one of these two text boxes:

Protection Password	Requires a password to open the file.
Write Reservation Password	Requires a password to save the file.

6. When prompted, retype the password and press Enter to confirm.

7. Click OK to close the Save As dialog box.

If you are adding a password to a file you have saved before, you are prompted to confirm replacing the file. Click on the Yes button.

Write down The password in a safe place.

Entering Summary Information

By default, Excel prompts you for summary information about the workbook. Here you can enter the author's name, comments about the workbook, key words that indicate the contents, and so on. After you save the file once, you won't be prompted for summary information again. To add or edit the summary information, follow these steps:

1. Select the File Summary Info command. You see the Summary Info dialog box.

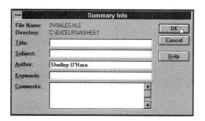

2. Make entries in any of the following text boxes: Title, Subject, Author, Keywords, Comments.

135

3. Click OK.

Turning Off the Prompt for Summary Information

If you don't like to be prompted for this summary information, you can turn off the prompt. You can still add the summary information at any time by selecting the File Summary Info command. To turn off the prompt for summary information, follow these steps:

1. Select the Tools Options command.

2. Select the General tab. You see the General tab of the Options dialog box.

Uncheck this check box.

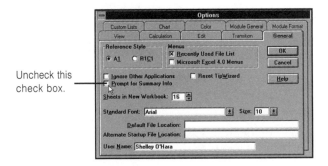

3. Uncheck the Prompt for Summary Info check box.

4. Click OK.

Saving an Excel File in Another Format

If you need to share files with someone who doesn't have Excel, you can save the file in another format. Here are the formats Excel supports:

Formatted Text (Separated by spaces)

Text (Separated with tabs)

CSV (Separated with commas)

Excel 4.0 Workbook

Excel 4.0, 3.0, or 2.1 Worksheet

1-2-3 Release 3.x files (with or without formatting files: WK3, FM3, WK3)

1-2-3 Release 2.x files (with or without formatting files: WK1, FMT, WK1, ALL, WK1)

1-2-3 Release 1.x files (WKS)

Quattro Pro DOS (WQ1)

dBASE IV, III, or II

Text (Mac, OS/2, or DOS)

CSV (Mac, OS/2, or DOS)

DIF (Data Interchange Format)

SYLK (Symbolic Link)

To save the file in a different format, follow these steps:

1. If you are saving the file for the first time, select the File Save command. If you have saved and named the file once and want to add a password, select the File Save As command. The Save As dialog box appears.

2. Select the appropriate drive and directory.

3. Type a file name in the File Name text box.

4. Click on the down arrow next to the Save File as Type drop-down list and click on a file type. If necessary, click on the scroll arrows to scroll through the list. If the file type you need isn't listed, try an intermediary file type. For instance, most other spreadsheet programs can import text or CSV files.

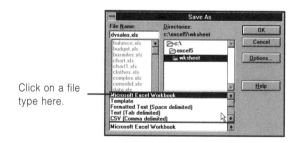

Click on a file type here.

5. Click OK. Excel saves the workbook in the selected format.

Cheat Sheet

Opening a Workbook

1. Click the Open button ▭.
2. Select the drive and directory.
3. Double-click on the file you want to open.

Creating a New Workbook

- Click the New Workbook button ▭.

  OR
- Select File New.

  OR
- Press Ctrl+N.

Opening Multiple Workbooks

1. Click the Open button ▭.
2. Select the workbook you want to open.
3. Repeat steps 1 and 2 until all the workbooks you want to use are open.

Displaying Multiple Workbooks

1. Select Window Arrange.
2. Click on an arrangement.
3. Click OK.

Switching Among Workbooks

1. Select Window.
2. Click the window you want to make active.

Freezing Panes

1. Select the cell where you want to freeze the panes.
2. Select the Window Freeze Pane commands.

21

Opening a Workbook

When you start Excel, a blank workbook is displayed. That's fine if you want to create a new workbook, but what if you want to work on a workbook you created and saved previously? You can open previously saved files with the File Open command. And you can create a new workbook at any time using the File New command.

Basic Survival

Opening a Workbook

When you want to display on-screen a file you've saved before, use the File Open command. Opening a file reads the information from the disk and displays it on-screen. Once the file is opened, you can make any changes you want.

To open a workbook, follow these steps:

1. Select the File Open command or click on the Open button [icon]. You see the Open dialog box.

Click on a file name in this list.

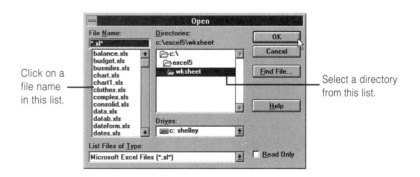

Select a directory from this list.

2. If the file is on another drive, display the Drives drop-down list and click on the drive.

3. If the file is in another directory, select the directory in the Directories list. Excel displays the workbooks in the selected directory and drive.

4. Double-click on the file you want to open. Or highlight the file and press Enter or click OK. Excel displays the workbook on-screen.

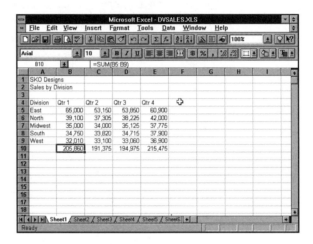

To open one of the four files you've used most recently, click on the File menu. The last four files you opened are listed; click on the one you want.

$Ctrl + O$
opens a file

If you can't find the file you want to open, use Excel's Find File feature, described in Chapter 41, "Using Find File."

Creating a New Workbook

As mentioned, Excel displays a new blank workbook each time you start the program. You can also create a new workbook at any time by selecting the File New command or by clicking on the New Workbook button.

Beyond Survival

Opening Multiple Workbooks

Just as you can have many pieces of paper on your desk, you can have several workbooks open at once in Excel. Open the first workbook you want using the File Open command. Then select the command again to open the next workbook. The number of worksheets that you can have open depends on the computer memory you have.

Once the workbooks are open, you can choose to display all of them, switch among them, and copy and paste information from one workbook to the next.

Displaying Multiple Workbooks

The last workbook you opened will be displayed on the top of the stack. To display all open windows, follow these steps:

1. Select the Window Arrange command, and the Arrange Windows dialog box appears.

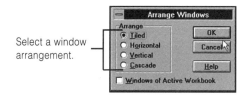

Select a window arrangement.

2. Click on an arrangement:

Tiled	Displays the windows in small areas on-screen.
Horizontal	Displays the windows in even panes horizontally across the screen.
Vertical	Displays the windows in even panes vertically on-screen.
Cascade	Stacks the windows one on top of the other with the title bars all showing.

3. Click OK. Excel arranges the windows according to your choice. In the following figure, the windows are tiled.

Maximize button

Tiled windows

To maximize a window so that it fills the entire screen, click the Maximize button in the workbook title bar.

Switching Among Workbooks

To switch among open workbooks, click on the worksheet you want. If you can't see the worksheet, follow these steps:

1. Select the Window menu. At the bottom of this menu, there is a list of open windows; the workbook with the check mark is the active one.

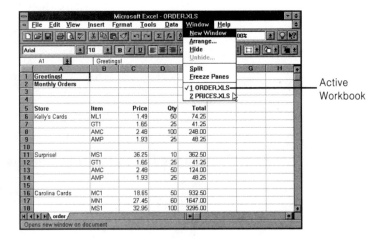

Active Workbook

2. Click on the workbook you want to make active. Excel switches to that workbook window.

Opening the Same Workbook in Two Windows

When you have extremely large workbooks, or you want to view more than one worksheet from the same workbook, you might want to display different parts in different windows. For example, you can display the top part of the workbook in one window and the bottom part in another window. To do so, follow these steps:

1. Select the Window New Window command. Excel opens a second copy of the workbook and displays the number 2 after the workbook name.

2. Arrange the windows so you can see both, as described in an earlier section.

3. Scroll to display what you want in the first window. Then move to the second window and scroll to display what you want in this window.

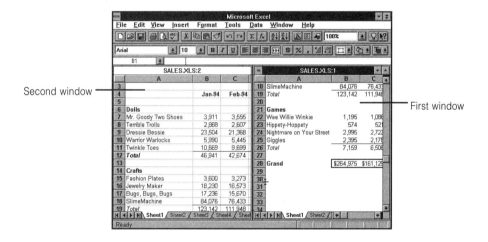

Second window —

First window —

Freezing Panes

Another feature that's handy for use with extremely large worksheets is the Freeze Panes command. For instance, suppose that you have a worksheet with monthly and quarterly sales across the columns and products down the rows. When you are looking at the later months or the products at the bottom, you won't be able to tell which row and column you are in. To fix this problem, you can freeze the column and row headings on-screen so that no matter where you scroll, the headings tell you what row and column you are in.

To freeze panes, follow these steps:

1. Select the cell where you want to freeze the panes. To freeze just the row headings, select the cell in the top row and in the column to the right of the one you want to freeze. To freeze just the column headings, select the cell in the first column and in the row immediately below the row headings you want to freeze. To freeze both the row and column headings, select the cell immediately below and to the right of the rows and columns you want to freeze.

You want to freeze these row headings.

You want to freeze these column headings.

Active cell for freeze

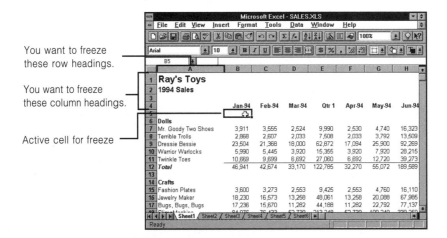

2. Select the Window Freeze Pane commands. Word displays a single line for row or column freezes and four lines when you freeze both. Now you can scroll through the worksheet, and the headings remain.

Notice the skip in column letters.

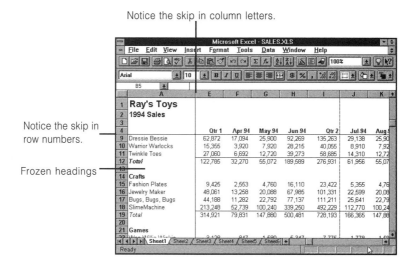

Notice the skip in row numbers.

Frozen headings

Opening a Non-Excel File

If you share data with someone who does not have Excel, you may need to convert and open different file types. For instance, say you need to get some files from a friend who uses 1-2-3. Before you can use those files, you'll need to convert them to Excel's format. With Excel, you can open different file types by following these steps:

1. Select the File Open command. You see the Open dialog box.

2. If the file is on another drive, display the Drives drop-down list and click on the drive.

3. If the file is in another directory, click on the directory in the Directories list.

4. Click on the down arrow next to the List Files of Type drop-down list to see the list of acceptable file types.

5. Click on the file type you want to open. Excel will then list files of that type in the file list.

145

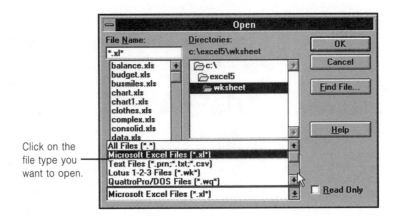

Click on the
file type you
want to open.

6. **Double-click on the file** you want to open. Excel opens the file.
Depending on the file type, you may need to do some formatting
to make the worksheet like you want it to look.

PART 3

Formatting and Printing a Worksheet

If your worksheet is just a jumble of numbers, your readers probably aren't going to pay much attention to it. To create a worksheet that is professional and attractive, you need to spend some time formatting the data. Formatting means to change the appearance of the worksheet, and can include making entries bold, adding a border around a group of key values, making certain columns wider, and more. Part 3 focuses on putting the finishing touches on the worksheet and then printing it. The following topics are covered:

- Formatting Data
- Aligning Data
- Changing the Number Format
- Changing the Column Width
- Changing the Row Height
- Adding Borders, Patterns, and Color
- Protecting Data
- Copying Formatting and Creating Styles
- Using AutoFormat
- Setting Up the Page
- Adding Headers and Footers
- Previewing a Worksheet
- Printing a Worksheet

Cheat Sheet

Understanding Fonts

- A font is a set of characters and numbers that look the same.
- Fonts can come in different styles and sizes.

Making Entries Bold, Italic, and Underlined

1. Select the cell or range to change.
2. Click on one of the following buttons:

   Bold   **B**

   Italic   *I*

   Underline   <u>U</u>

Changing the Font with the Formatting Toolbar

1. Select the range to change.
2. Click the down arrow next to the Font list.
3. Click the font you want.

Changing the Font Size with the Formatting Toolbar

1. Select the range to change.
2. Click the down arrow next to the Size list.
3. Click the size you want.

Undoing Formatting

1. Select the cell or range to clear.
2. Select Edit Clear Formats.

22

Formatting Data

Certain values in your worksheet may be more important than others and you may want these to stand out. For example, so that readers understand what each row and column means, you may want to make the headings bold or italic. You can also change the font or type style of the text. Selecting an appropriate font is one way to convey a subtle impression in your worksheet.

Basic Survival

Understanding Fonts

A *font* is a set of characters and numbers in a certain style. Some fonts are professional and business-like, such as Times New Roman and Avant Garde. Some fonts are decorative and ornate, such as *Zapf Chancery* and *Brush Script*. Some fonts are actually a set of symbols. You can use symbol fonts to insert special characters in your document (_°¬¿).

In addition to their appearance, fonts have other characteristics that set them apart; in particular, fonts can come in different styles (**bold**, *italic*, and <u>underline</u>) and sizes. Sizes are measured in points; there are 72 points in one inch. In addition to changing the font, you can select a different style and size.

Where do you get fonts? And what determines which fonts you have? You can get fonts from the following sources:

- Your printer will determine some of the fonts you have. Different printers come with different fonts. With some printers, you can add additional fonts, usually by adding a font cartridge. In the font list, you can tell which fonts are printer fonts because they have a little printer icon next to them.

- You may also have TrueType fonts. Windows provides a font technology called TrueType; TrueType fonts are installed through Windows and stored in files on your hard disk. These files tell the printer how to create the particular font. In the font list, TrueType fonts are indicated with TT.

- Some programs come with a set of fonts. These fonts, also stored in files, are available for your use.

Making Entries Bold, Italic, and Underlined

Bold, italic, and underline are three of the most common style changes. Excel conveniently provides buttons for these features on the Formatting toolbar. You can use these buttons to quickly make a cell or range of cells bold, italic, or underlined. To do so, follow these steps:

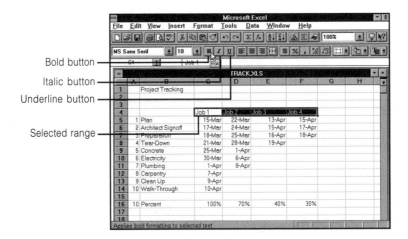

1. Select the cell or range you want to change.

2. Click on one of the following buttons:

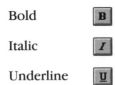

Bold	**B**
Italic	*I*
Underline	U

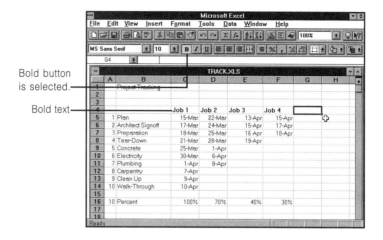

Bold button
is selected.

Bold text

*Click Toolbar
buTTons To
Turn
formaTTing
on or off*

Excel formats the selected range accordingly. Note that the button appears to be pressed when the formatting option is selected. The following figure shows examples of bold, italic, and underline.

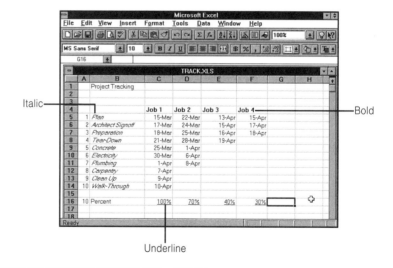

Italic

Bold

Underline

Changing the Font with the Formatting Toolbar

Another way to make headings stand out is to change the font. As mentioned, different fonts have different looks and can convey slightly different meanings. You can use the toolbar to quickly change the font. Follow these steps:

1. Select the range you want to change.

2. Click on the down arrow next to the Font list. You see a drop-down list of font choices. Your list will vary depending on the fonts you have on your computer and printer.

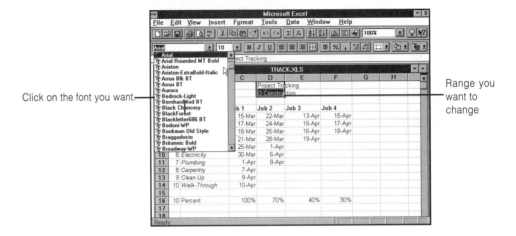

Click on the font you want

Range you want to change

3. Click on the font you want. Excel makes the font change.

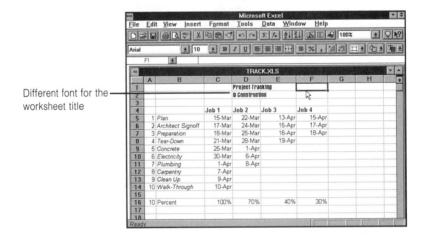

Different font for the worksheet title

Changing the Font Size with the Formatting Toolbar

Excel uses a small point size for all entries you type—usually 10-point type. This size might be appropriate for the data in your worksheet, but you may want to make the worksheet titles or row and column headings larger. The quickest way to change the font size is to use the toolbar. Follow these steps:

1. Select the range you want to change.

2. Click on the down arrow next to the Size list.

Click on the
size you want.

Range you
want to change.

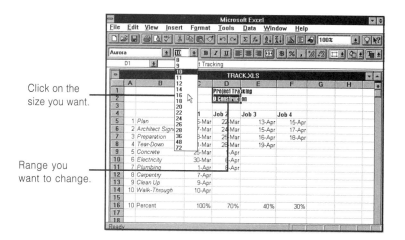

3. Click on the size you want. Excel formats the range with the new size. If necessary, Excel also adjusts the row height.

16-point title

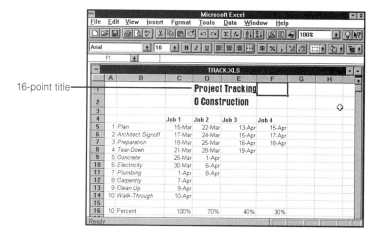

Beyond Survival

Undoing Formatting

If you make a change and realize immediately that you don't like it, you can undo it with the Edit Undo command. You can turn off bold, italic, and underline by selecting the range and then clicking the appropriate button again.

If you want to clear all formatting from a cell or range of cells, follow these steps:

1. Select the cell or range you want to clear.

2. Select the Edit Clear Formats command. Excel clears all the applied formatting.

Changing the Font with the Font Tab

If you want to make several changes or if you want to preview the formatting before you apply it to a cell or range, you can use the Format Cells command. The Format Cells dialog box enables you to select the font, size, and style all at once. You can also view a preview. Some options, such as underline styles and strikethrough, are available only through the dialog box. To change the font with the Format Cells command, follow these steps:

1. Select the cell or range you want to change.

Ctrl + 1 = Format Cells

2. Select the Format Cells command.

3. Click on the Font tab. You see the Font tab of the Format Cells dialog box.

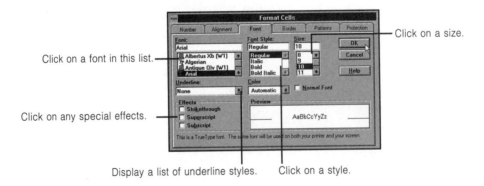

Click on a font in this list.

Click on any special effects.

Display a list of underline styles.

Click on a style.

Click on a size.

4. In the Font list, click on the font you want.

5. In the Size list, click on the size you want.

6. If you want to change the style, click on a style from the Font Style list.

7. If you want any special effects, check the check box for any of these special effects:

Strikethrough

Superscript

Subscript

8. If you want to use a different type of underline, display the Under-line drop-down list, and then click on the underline style you want.

9. When you are finished making changes, click on the OK button. Excel formats the selected range with the options you selected.

For information on changing the color, see Chapter 27 "Adding Borders, Patterns, and Color."

Formatting Tips

When you are formatting data, consider the following formatting shortcuts:

- If you use the same font, size, and style over and over again, consider creating a *style*. With a style, you can save the formatting of a particular cell and then apply that style quickly to other cells. See Chapter 29, "Copying Formatting and Creating Styles."

- You can copy the font formatting used in one cell to another cell or range. See Chapter 29, "Copying Formatting and Creating Styles."

- Excel provides some AutoFormats that you can use if your worksheet is set up in a table format. See Chapter 30, "Using AutoFormat."

Cheat Sheet

Using the Alignment Buttons

1. Select the cell or range to change.
2. Click one of the buttons in the Formatting toolbar:

   Center

   Align Left

   Align Right

Centering Across Columns

1. Select the range that contains the heading and the range that you want to center across.
2. Click the Center Across Columns button .

Wrapping Text

1. Type the text into the cell.
2. Select Format Cells.
3. Click the Alignment tab.
4. Check the Wrap Text check box.
5. Click OK.

Changing the Top to Bottom Alignment or Orientation

1. Select the cell or range to align.
2. Select Format Cells.
3. Select the Alignment tab.
4. Click on a horizontal alignment.
5. Click on a vertical alignment.
6. Click on an orientation.
7. Click OK.

23

Aligning Data

Think of aligning data as straightening up the worksheet, putting everything in its proper place. Excel provides many alignment features. You can align one cell across a range, which is perfect for worksheet titles. You can align an entry horizontally (left to right) within the cell. And you can align cells vertically (top to bottom). For a special effect, you can change the orientation of cells.

Basic Survival

Using the Alignment Buttons

By default, all numbers align to the right, and all text aligns to the left. If you keep this alignment, your columns may not be balanced: column headings for numbers will be to the left and numbers will be to the right. Instead of leaving headings misaligned, change the alignment. For example, centered or right-aligned headings work best over columns of numbers.

Headings don't align over the columns of numbers.

	Microsoft Excel					
File	**Edit**	**View**	**Insert**	**Format**	**Tools**	**Data** **Window** **Help**

Arial | 10

F1

PRODSALE.XLS

	A	B	C	D	E	F
1	Ball Corporation					
2	Quarterly Sales Report					
3						
4						
5	Product	Qtr 1	Qtr 2	Qtr 3	Qtr 4	
6	Soccer	53300	53150	53850	186750	
7	Basketball	36650	36950	39500	136350	
8	Football	37100	37305	38225	131425	
9	Baseball	35925	36125	36820	126185	
10	Volleyballs	33700	33820	34715	119190	
11	Other	31900	33100	33060	114300	
12	TOTAL	230575	232450	236170	814200	
13						
14						
15						
16						

Sheet1 / Sheet2 / Sheet3 / Sheet4 / Sheet5 / Shee

Ready

Excel provides three alignment buttons on the Formatting toolbar:
Align Left, Center, and Align Right . You can use these buttons to
quickly change the alignment. Follow these steps:

1. Select the cell or range you want to change.

2. Click on one of the following buttons in the Formatting toolbar:

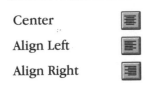

Center

Align Left

Align Right

To undo an
alignment
change, click
another
alignment
button

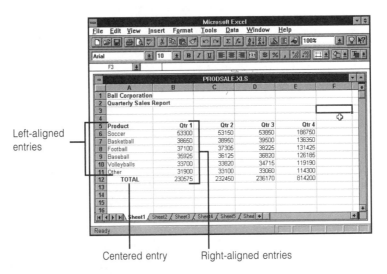

Left-aligned
entries

Centered entry   Right-aligned entries

Centering Across Columns

Suppose that you want a worksheet title to appear above the rows and
columns of the worksheet data. If you enter a worksheet title in cell A1,
the title isn't centered over the data. You can try to enter the title in a
different column in that row, but it probably isn't going to line up
exactly. Instead, center the entry across columns by following these
steps:

1. Select the range that contains the heading and the range that you
want to center across.

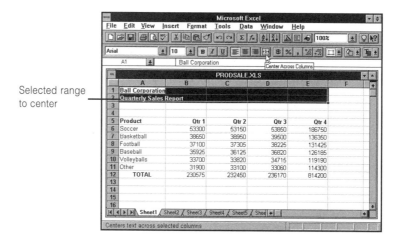

Selected range
to center

2. Click on the Center Across Columns button.

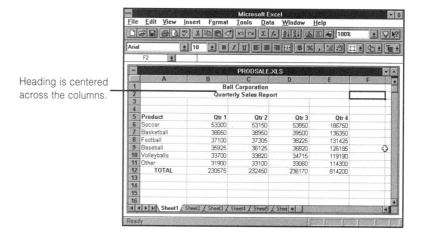

Heading is centered
across the columns.

ImporTanT!   Keep in mind that when you center a heading across columns, the
entry remains in the original cell, although it may not appear that way.
To edit that entry, you must select the original cell.

Beyond Survival

Wrapping Text   Sometimes you may want to include a lot of text within a cell. But
when you type past the cell boundaries, Excel just spills the text over
onto the other cells, and you have one long line of text. Instead, you
can choose to wrap the text in the cell by following these steps:

1. Type the text into the cell.

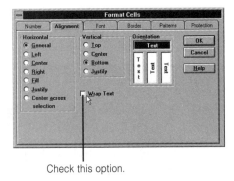

Text you want to wrap

2. Select the Format Cells command.

3. Click on the Alignment tab. You see the Alignment tab of the Format Cells dialog box.

4. Check the Wrap Text check box.

Check this option.

5. Click OK, and Word wraps the text within the cell and adjusts the row height.

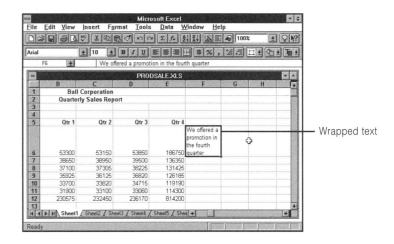

Wrapped text

Changing the Top to Bottom Alignment or Orientation

Aligning entries left-to-right and across columns are common alignment changes. In addition to those, Excel offers a few other fancy alignment choices. You can choose to align the entries with the top or in the center of the cell. And you can change the orientation so that the entry reads top to bottom or bottom to top. To use either of these options, follow these steps:

1. Select the cell or range you want to align.

2. Select the Format Cells command.

3. Select the Alignment tab. You see the Alignment tab of the Format Cells dialog box.

4. In the Horizontal area, click on horizontal alignment: General, Left, Right, Center, Justify, or Fill.

5. In the Vertical area, click on vertical alignment: Top, Center, Bottom, Justify.

6. In the Orientation area, click on an orientation.

7. Click OK, and Excel makes the change.

163

Cheat Sheet

Changing the Number Format Using the Toolbar

1. Select the cell or range to change.
2. Click a style button.
3. If necessary, change the number of decimal places by clicking the Increase Decimal ⊞ or Decrease Decimal ⊞ button.

Changing the Number Format by Command

1. Select the cell or range to change.
2. Select Format Cells.
3. Click the Number tab.
4. Click the category you want.
5. Click the style you want.
6. Click OK.

Creating a Custom Format

1. Select the cell or range to change.
2. Select Format Cells.
3. Click the Number tab.
4. Click the category you want.
5. Click a style that is closest to the one you want to create.
6. Edit the codes.
7. Click OK.

24

Changing the Number Format

How a number is formatted often changes its meaning: 67%, $67, and .67 all mean different things. In your worksheet, you need to apply the appropriate number format so that the meaning of the numbers in your worksheet is clear.

Basic Survival

Changing the Number Format Using the Toolbar

When you enter a number in Excel, it's just a plain number—6700.88, for instance. You can change the number format to more accurately reflect the cell contents. Take a look at the following worksheet. Notice that it is difficult to make sense of the numbers when they are all formatted the same.

Numbers before formatting —

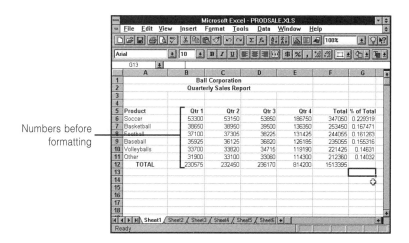

If you want to use currency, comma, or percent format, you can use the buttons on the Formatting toolbar. Follow these steps:

1. Select the cell or range you want to change.

2. Click on a style button:

Currency Style $\boxed{\$}$

Percent Style $\boxed{\%}$

Comma Style $\boxed{,}$

3. If necessary, change the number of decimal places that are displayed by clicking on the Increase Decimal $\boxed{\substack{+.0 \\ .00}}$ or Decrease Decimal $\boxed{\substack{.00 \\ +.0}}$ buttons.

means you should widen The column

Excel applies the appropriate number format, as shown in the following figure.

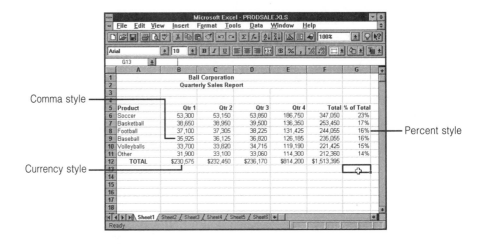

Changing the Number Format by Command

Excel provides many number styles to choose from. If you want to use a style other than comma, currency, or percent, you can use the Format Cells command to select a style. Not only does this command give you access to many other styles, it also enables you to preview the style before you make the change. To use the command method, follow these steps:

1. Select the cell or range you want to change.

2. Select the Format Cells command.

3. Click on the Number tab. You see the Number tab of the Format Cells dialog box.

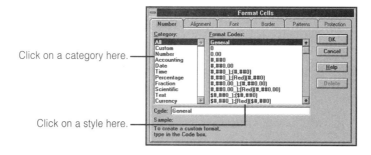

Click on a category here. —

Click on a style here. —

4. In the Category list, click on the category you want.

5. In the Format Codes list, click on the style you want.

6. Click OK, and Excel makes the change. The following figure shows examples of different styles.

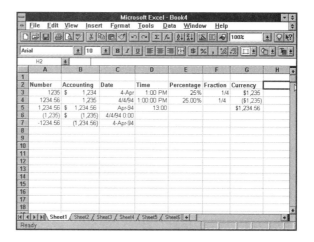

Beyond Survival

Entering a Number Format As You Type the Entry

Another way to specify the number format you want is to type it the way you want. You can include the following characters in a cell entry to specify a particular format:

$ Currency style

,   Comma style

%   Percent style

167

Excel will apply the appropriate format when you type the symbol or character.

Creating a Custom Format

If none of the predefined formats fits your needs, you can create your own custom format. For instance, you may want to use the format - 0 - for zero entries. If so, you can create a custom number format. Before you begin, you need to understand the parts of a number format.

In a number format, you can include up to four parts: a positive number format, a negative number format, a format for zeroes, and a format for text. Each part is separated by a semicolon. Within each part, a code is used to represent digits. Here are some common codes and their meanings:

Code	Meaning
#	Placeholder for digits. If the digit is a non-significant zero, it is not displayed.
0	Placeholder for digits. Zeroes are displayed. (For example, 6.5 in the format #.00 would display as 6.50.)
?	Placeholder for digits. Uses a space for non-significant zeroes.
.	Decimal point.
,	Thousands separator.
%	Percent sign. Excel multiplies the entry by 100.
;	Separates positive number format from negative number format.
Underline	Skips the width of the next character. Use this to align positive numbers and negative numbers displayed in parentheses.
"text"	Displays text entered within double quotation marks.
[Red]	Indicates color selection.

To create a custom code, start with a similar code and then edit it to match the custom code you want to create. Follow these steps:

1. Select the cell or range you want to change.

2. Select the Format Cells command.

3. Click on the Number tab. You see the Number tab of the Format Cells dialog box.

4. In the Category list, click on the category you want.

5. In the Format Codes list, click on the style that comes closest to the one you want to create.

6. In the Code text box, edit the code so that it formats the numbers as you want them to appear.

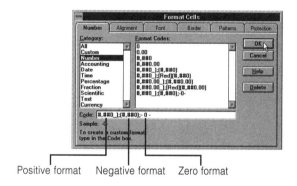

Positive format   Negative format   Zero format

7. Click OK. Excel creates the custom code.

To apply a custom code to other cells or ranges, display the Number tab and then click on Custom in the Category list. The format code you defined will be listed with this category. Click on it and then click OK.

Cannot delete built-in formats

To delete a custom code, display the Number tab and click on Custom in the Category list. Then click on the Delete button. Keep in mind that you cannot delete any of Excel's built-in formats.

Cheat Sheet

What Happens When an Entry Won't Fit

- A long entry will appear to spill over into adjacent columns.
- If the next column contains an entry, Excel truncates the display of the long entry.
- If a number is too big to fit in a cell, Excel displays number signs (###) in the cell.

Using the Mouse to Widen a Column

1. Point to the right column heading border.
2. Drag to a new width.
3. When the column is the right width, release the mouse button.

Adjusting Columns Automatically

- Double-click the right column border.
  OR
- Select Format Column AutoFit Selection.

Using the Column Width Dialog Box

1. Select the column(s) you want to change.
2. Select Format Column Width.
3. Type a new value.
4. Click OK.

Using the Worksheet default Column Width

1. Select Format Column Standard Width.
2. Type a new width.
3. Click OK.

25

Changing the Column Width

When you create a new worksheet, all columns have the same width. However, using the same column width throughout probably isn't going to be very practical. Some columns may contain more information and need to be wider, and some columns may need to be narrower. Or you may want more room between columns. If so, change the column width.

Basic Survival

**What Happens
When an Entry
Won't Fit**

When you enter a long text entry, the entry will appear to spill over into adjacent columns. (The entry is really in one cell, but it is displayed across several columns.) If the next column contains an entry, however, Excel truncates the display of the long entry. The cell still contains the entire entry, but you can see only the first part of it.

When you enter a number that is too big to fit in a cell, Excel applies the scientific number style. If you format a number and it is too big to fit in a cell, Excel displays number signs (###) in the cell. In either case, you need to adjust the column width.

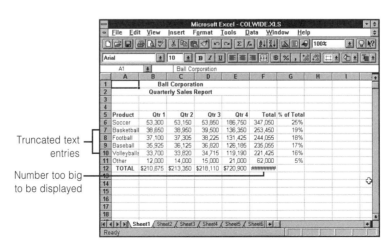

Truncated text entries

Number too big to be displayed

Using the Mouse to Widen a Column

The easiest way to change the column width is to use the mouse. Using this method, you can visually see the changes. When the column is as wide as you want, you can quit dragging. Follow these steps:

1. **Point to the right column heading border.** The pointer will change to a thick line with arrows on either side of it. This indicates the pointer is in the right spot.

2. **Click and hold down the mouse button, and drag** to a new width. As you drag, you will see an outline of the column border. A measurement of the width also appears in the reference area of the formula bar.

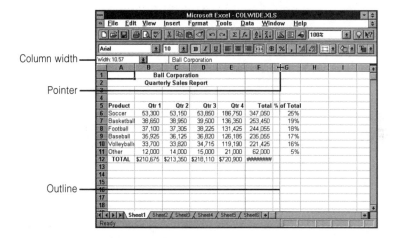

3. **When the column is as wide as you want, release the mouse button.** Excel adjusts the width.

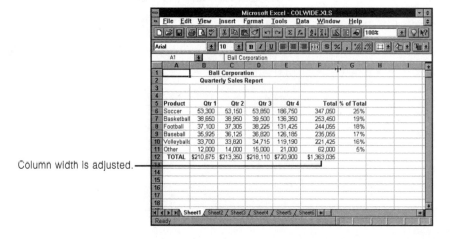

You can change the width of several columns at once by selecting the columns you want to change, and then dragging one column border to change them all.

Adjusting Columns Automatically

ShorTcuT: double-click righT column border nexT To column leTTer

If you don't want to change each column's width individually, you can have Excel adjust the column width to fit the largest entry in that column. To do so, double-click the right column border next to the column letter, or select the cell with the largest entry and select the Format Column AutoFit Selection command.

Beyond Survival

Using the Column Width Dialog Box

If you want to enter an exact value for the column width, use the command method. Follow these steps:

1. Select the column or columns you want to change.

2. Select the Format Column Width command. The Column Width dialog box appears.

3. Type a new value. The value you enter should reflect the number of digits that will fit in the column.

Type the value here.

4. Click OK, and Excel adjusts the column width.

Using the Worksheet Default Column Width

If you change the column width and then want to return to the worksheet default width, you can do so. The worksheet default column width is 8.43 characters in the worksheet default font and size. Follow these steps to return to the original setting:

1. Select the Format Column Standard Width command. You will see the Standard Width dialog box.

2. If you want to change the default width, type a new width. To accept the standard width, skip this step.

3. Click OK. Excel adjusts all columns in the worksheet that have not previously been changed. This command affects all selected worksheets, but does not affect new worksheets.

Cheat Sheet

Using the Mouse to Adjust Row Height

1. Point to the border below the row number you want to change.
2. Drag up or down.
3. Release the mouse button.

Using AutoFit

- Double-click the bottom row border.
  OR
- Select Format Row AutoFit.

Changing Row Height Using Commands

1. Select the row(s) to change.
2. Select Format Row.
3. Select Height.
4. Type the value you want.
5. Click OK.

26

Changing the Row Height

When you change the font, Excel automatically adjusts the row height so that the font fits. But just as you can adjust column width, you can adjust the row height. For example, you might want to have more room between some or all of the rows in your worksheet.

Basic Survival

Using the Mouse to Adjust Row Height

Using the mouse, you can visually adjust the row height by dragging the row border. Follow these steps:

1. Click on the border below the row number that you want to change. The pointer will change to a thick vertical line with arrows on either side of it. This indicates the pointer is in the right spot.

2. Drag up or down to change the height. As you drag, you see an outline of the row border. The row height appears in the reference area of the formula bar.

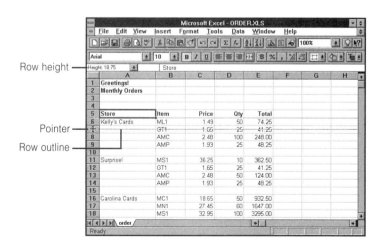

Row height

Pointer

Row outline

175

3. Release the mouse button. Excel adjusts the row.

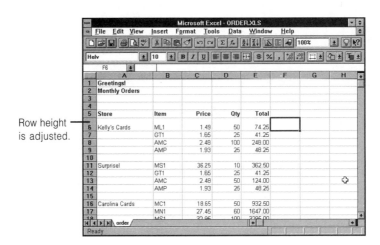

Row height is adjusted.

You can change the height of several rows at once by selecting the rows you want to change, and then dragging or using the command to change the height of one.

If you drag the bottom border of a row past the top border, you hide the row. See Chapter 28, "Protecting Data" for more information on hiding rows.

Using AutoFit

ShorTcuT: double-click The boTTom row border

Excel will adjust the row height automatically when you change the font. If you enter a custom row height and then decide to go back to the original height, you can have Excel adjust the row height for the best fit. Simply double-click the bottom row border, or select the Format Row AutoFit command.

Beyond Survival

Changing the Row Height Using Commands

Sometimes getting the mouse pointer in the right spot to drag the row is difficult. If you prefer, you can use the command method. In addition, if you use the commands, you can enter an exact value for the row height. Follow these steps:

1. Select the row or rows that you want to change.

2. Select the Format Row command; a submenu of choices appears.

3. Select the Height command. You see the Row Height dialog box.

Type the value here.

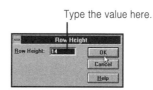

4. Type the value you want (measured in points). The default value will depend on the font size.

5. Click OK.

Cheat Sheet

Adding a Border with the Toolbar

1. Select the range to which you want to add a border.
2. Click the Borders button .

Adding a Pattern

1. Select the cell or range to change.
2. Select Format Cells.
3. Select the Patterns tab.
4. Click the down arrow next to the Pattern drop-down list and select a pattern.
5. Click OK.

Changing the Color

1. Select the cell or range to change.
2. Click the Font Color button to change the text or the Color button to change the background.
3. Click a color in the palette.

Using the Border Tab

1. Select the cell or range you want to change.
2. Select Format Cells.
3. Click the Border tab.
4. Click the border you want.
5. Click a border style in the Style list.
6. Click the down arrow next to the Color list, and then click on the color you want.
7. Click OK.

27

Adding Borders, Patterns, and Color

If you want to highlight certain sections of your worksheet, you can add a border or a pattern. You can also change the color of the text or the cell background. For example, you may want to add a border under your row headings to make them stand out, or you may want to shade a key section of the worksheet. With Excel, you can add borders, patterns, and colors easily.

Basic Survival

Adding a Border with the Toolbar

Borders are a good way to indicate key information in a worksheet. You may want to underline the totals or put an outline around a key column of data. Follow these steps to add a border:

1. Select the range to which you want to add a border.

2. Click on the Borders button [image]. A drop-down list of common borders appears. From this palette, you can select both the side you want to border and the line style you want to use by clicking on an appropriate style.

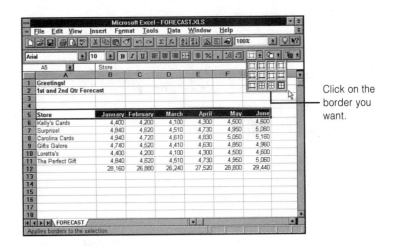

Click on the border you want.

Excel applies the border to the selected cells.

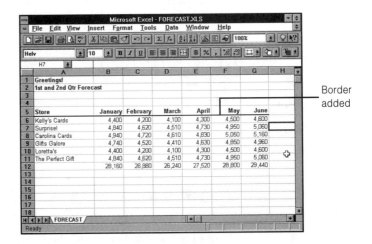

Border added

Click Borders buTTon To apply The lasT border selecTed

To remove a border, select the range again. Click on the Borders button and then click on the None option. Excel removes the border. Remember that a cell can contain a border to the left or right and top or bottom. If you can't find the border to turn off, try selecting the cell next to, above, or below the cell you *think* has the border.

Adding a Pattern

Patterns are also good for adding emphasis. An easy way to separate rows in a database, for example, is to apply a pattern to every other row. Follow these steps to apply a pattern to a cell or range of cells.

1. Select the cell or range you want to change.

2. Select the Format Cells command.

3. Select the Patterns tab to access the Patterns tab of the Format Cells dialog box.

4. Click on the down arrow next to the Pattern drop-down list and select a pattern.

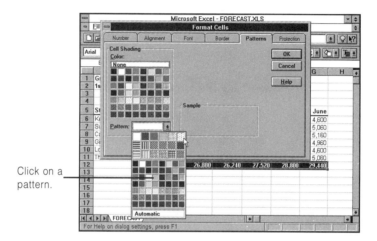

Click on a pattern.

5. Click OK, and Excel applies the pattern.

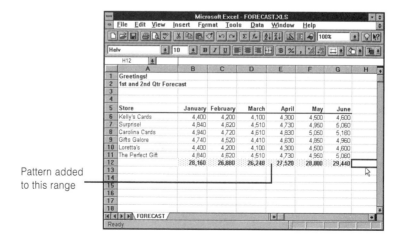

Pattern added to this range

181

You can also apply a colored pattern using the Color button, as described next.

Changing the Font Color

Another way to add emphasis is to add color. You can change the color of the cell's contents or the color of the cell's background (covered in the next section). The quickest way to change colors is to use the Color and Font Color buttons on the Formatting toolbar.

Remember when changing colors that data that appears in color on-screen will print in color only if you have a color printer. To change the text color, follow these steps:

1. Select the cell or range you want to change.

2. Click on the Font Color button to see a palette of available colors.

Range you want to change

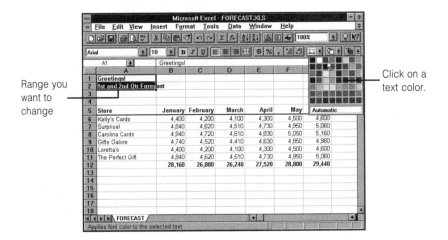

Click on a text color.

3. Click on a color in the palette. Excel changes the text color.

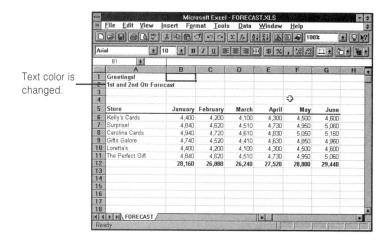

Text color is changed.

Changing the Background Color

To change the background color, follow these steps:

1. Select the cell or range you want to change.

2. Select the Color button to see a palette of available colors.

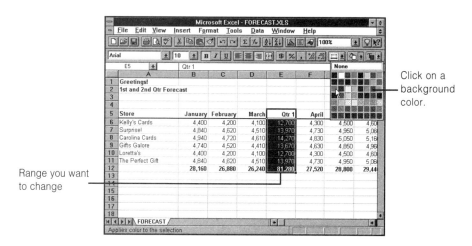

Click on a background color.

Range you want to change

Don't use The same color for TexT and background

3. Click on a color in the palette, and Excel applies the background color.

Beyond Survival

Using the Border Tab

If the Borders button doesn't include the line style you want, you can use a different method to add a border: the Border tab of the Format Cells dialog box. Using this dialog box, you can select which side you want the border to appear on and which style to use. Unlike the toolbar button, you can use the dialog box to change the color of the line as well. Follow these steps:

Sets The border and color aT The same Time

1. Select the cell or range you want to change.

2. Select the Format Cells command.

3. Click on the Border tab. You see the Border tab of the Format Cells dialog box.

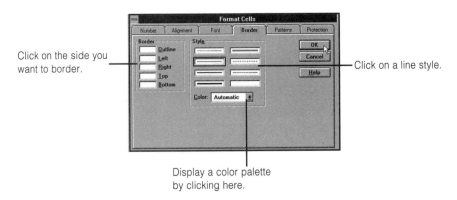

Click on the side you want to border.

Click on a line style.

Display a color palette by clicking here.

4. Click on the border you want: Outline (all sides), Top, Left, Right, Bottom.

5. Click on a border style in the Style list.

6. Click on the down arrow next to the Color list, and then click on the color you want.

7. Click OK. Excel applies the border.

Border and Color Tips

As you are working with borders, patterns, and colors, consider the following tips:

- If you use the toolbar buttons to select a border or color, the button remembers the last border or color settings you used. Therefore, you can select a range and click the button to apply the same border or color to another selection.

- If you want to keep the palette of borders or colors displayed, drag the palette off the toolbar. Then you can select from the palette.

- You can copy the border, pattern, or color formatting applied to a cell or range of cells using the Format Painter button. See Chapter 29, "Copying Formatting and Creating Styles," for more information on copying formatting.

Cheat Sheet

Hiding Columns and Rows

1. Select any cell in the column or row to hide.
2. Select Format Column Hide or Format Row Hide.

Unhiding Rows and Columns

1. Select the rows or columns on both sides of the hidden row or column.
2. Place the mouse pointer where the hidden row or column should appear.
3. Drag to unhide the column or row.

Protecting Cells

1. Select the cells you want to protect.
2. Select Format Cells.
3. Select the Protection tab.
4. Check the Locked check box and click OK.
5. Select Tools Protection.
6. Select Protect Sheet.
7. Type a password, and then type it again.
8. Click OK.
9. Select what you want protected.
10. Click OK.

Protecting the Workbook

1. Select Tools Protection.
2. Select Protect Workbook.
3. Type a password.
4. Click OK.
5. Select what you want protected.
6. Click OK.

28

Protecting Data

Worksheets can contain sensitive information that you may not want others to be able to see, access, or change. Excel provides several ways to protect the worksheet so that you can hide data you don't want others to see and you can protect data from change.

If you want to assign a password to a file so no one can open the file or save changes to it, see Chapter 20, "Saving and Closing a Workbook."

Basic Survival

Hiding Columns

Sometimes, it's a good idea to hide calculation columns or rows. For instance, suppose that you have the sales discount of an item in one column. This discount price is crucial to the next calculation, net sales, but doesn't really need to be displayed. You can hide the calculation column.

Hiding columns or rows prevents others from seeing them, but it is pretty easy to unhide the row or column. If you want to protect the data, see the other sections in this chapter.

Hidden elements don't print

To hide a column, follow these steps:

1. Select any cell in the column.

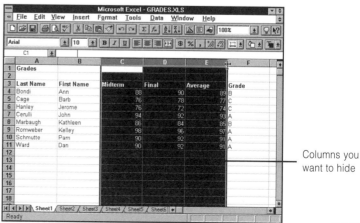

Columns you want to hide

2. Select the Format Column Hide command, or drag the right column border past the left border. Excel hides the columns. You know the columns are hidden because there is a jump in the column lettering.

CTrl + O To
hide a column

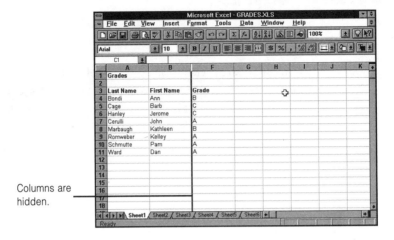

Columns are hidden.

Hiding Rows

To hide a row, follow these steps:

1. Select any cell in the row. If you want to hide several rows, select the ones you want to hide.

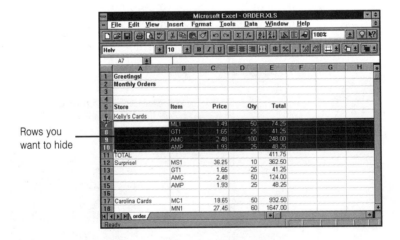

Rows you want to hide

2. Select the Format Row Hide command, or drag the bottom row border up past the top row border to hide the row. Excel hides the row. Notice that the row numbering reflects that some rows are hidden.

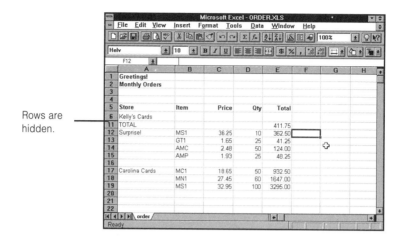

Rows are hidden.

$Ctrl + 9$ To hide a row

Be careful when dragging a row. It's easy to change the row height when you meant to hide the row instead.

Unhiding Rows and Columns

It's kind of tricky to unhide a row or column because you need a way to select the hidden row or column. You can use one of two methods:

- Select the rows or columns on both sides of the hidden row or column. For instance, if row 3 is hidden, select rows 2 and 4. Then select the Format Column Unhide command to unhide the column or the Format Row Unhide command to unhide rows.

- Place the mouse pointer where the hidden row or column should appear. You have to adjust the mouse pointer very carefully. When it is in the correct spot, it changes from a thick line to two thin lines, indicating that the hidden column is selected. Drag to unhide the column or row.

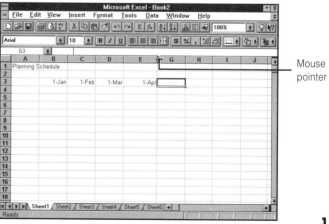

Mouse pointer

Hiding a Worksheet

Just as you can hide rows and columns, you can also hide worksheets that you don't want displayed. To hide a worksheet, follow these steps:

1. Select the sheet you want to hide.

2. Select the Format Sheet Hide command.

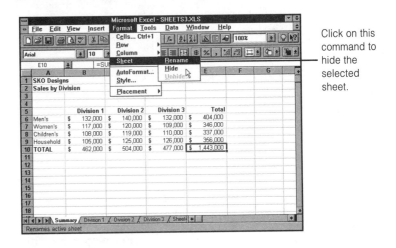

Click on this command to hide the selected sheet.

Unhiding a Worksheet

When you want to work on the hidden worksheet, you can unhide it. Follow these steps:

1. Select the Format Sheet Unhide command. You will see the Unhide dialog box, which lists all the hidden sheets.

2. Click on the sheet you want to unhide.

Click on the sheet you want to unhide.

3. Click OK, and Excel unhides the worksheet.

Although it is easy to hide and unhide worksheets, this technique won't provide much data security. If you are worried about someone else entering data or viewing data in a workbook, save it with a password. See Chapter 20, "Saving and Closing a Workbook," for more on passwords.

Protecting Cells

By default, all cells are locked, but the locking option has no effect unless worksheet protection is turned on. Once you turn on worksheet protection, locked cells cannot be changed or deleted. You can use these two features (cell locking and worksheet protection) to set up your worksheet. For example, you might set up the skeleton of a worksheet and then have someone else do the data entry. You can lock the cells that shouldn't be changed (for instance, those that contain formulas) and unlock the cells into which you want data entered.

Even if you have locked cells, another user could turn off worksheet protection and unlock the cells. If you are worried about this happening, assign a password. When you assign a password, that password is required to turn off the protection.

Make sure you get the cells locked or unlocked as you want them before you turn on worksheet protection. Once protection is on, you won't be able to make changes to the lock/unlock status unless you turn off protection.

Follow these steps to protect cells:

1. Select the cells that you want to protect.

2. Select the Format Cells command.

3. Select the Protection tab. You will see the Protection tab of the Format Cells dialog box.

When checked, the selected cells are locked.

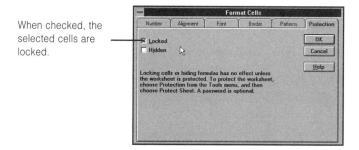

4. Check the Locked check box and click OK.

5. Select the Tools Protection command.

6. Select the Protect Sheet command. The Protect Sheet dialog box appears.

Type a password here.

7. If you want to assign a password to this sheet, type it and click OK. When prompted to confirm the password, retype it and click OK.

8. Select what you want protected: Contents, Objects, or Scenarios.

9. Click OK. Excel protects all the locked cells in the worksheet. If you try to change a locked cell, you will see the error message in the following figure.

Protecting the Workbook

In addition to protecting the worksheet, you can protect some aspects of the workbook—like the structure and the arrangement of the windows. Follow these steps:

1. Select the Tools Protection command.

2. Select the Protect Workbook command. You will see the Protect Workbook dialog box.

Type a password here.

3. If you want to assign a password to this workbook, type it and click OK. When prompted to retype the password, type it again and click OK.

4. Select what you want protected: Structure or Windows. If you select Structure, worksheets can't be added, moved, deleted, hidden, unhidden, or renamed. If you select Windows, windows can't be moved, sized, hidden, unhidden, or closed.

5. Click OK. Excel protects the workbook.

Cheat Sheet

Copying Formatting

1. Select the cells that contain the formatting you want to copy.
2. Click the Format Painter button.
3. Select the cells to copy the formatting to.

Creating a New Style by Example

1. Select a cell that is formatted with the attributes you want.
2. Select Format Style.
3. In the Style Name text box, type the style name.
4. If necessary, uncheck any of the Style Includes check boxes.
5. Click OK.

Using a Style

1. Select the range to format.
2. Select Format Style.
3. Click the down arrow next to the Style Name list.
4. Click the style you want.
5. Click OK.

Deleting a Style

1. Select Format Style.
2. Display the Style Name drop-down list, and then click on the style to delete.
3. Click the Delete button.

29

Copying Formatting and Creating Styles

Excel provides many timesaving formatting features. For example, if you get a range formatted just right and then want to use the same formatting on another range, you can copy the formatting. If you find yourself using the same formatting over and over, instead of copying it, you can create a *style*. A style is a set of predefined formats that you can create and then apply to a cell or range. For instance, if you often format data entries as bold, italic, and right-aligned, create a style that will assign these formats with a few clicks of the mouse.

Basic Survival

Copying Formatting

Copying a format is a quick way to save time and effort. Suppose you selected a range, added a border, changed the alignment, and used a different number format. You've got the range just how you want it. In fact, you like it so well that you want to format another range using the same formats. You don't have to re-create them, just copy them using the Format Painter button. Follow these steps:

1. Select the cells that contain the formatting you want to copy.

2. Click on the Format Painter button ![paintbrush icon]. The mouse pointer displays a little paintbrush next to the cross.

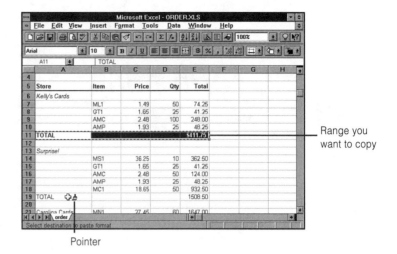

Range you want to copy

Pointer

3. Select the cells to which you want to copy the formatting. The formatting is applied to the selected range.

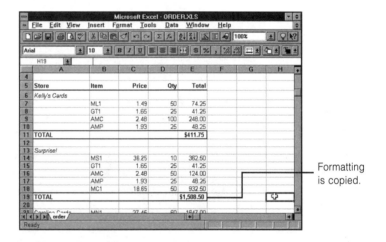

Formatting is copied.

Beyond Survival

Creating a New Style by Example

If you use the same set of formatting features often, you should consider creating a style. You can include the following formats in a style: number, font, alignment, border, patterns, and protection. The easiest way to create a new style is to base it on a cell or range you have formatted with the style elements you want. Follow these steps:

Apply
formatting
changes
first

1. Select a cell that is formatted with the attributes you want.

Formatting to copy

2. Select the Format Style command to access the Style dialog box.

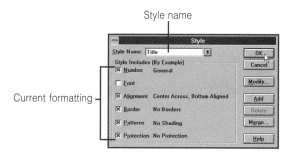

3. In the Style Name text box, type the style name. Notice that Excel updates the dialog box to reflect the formatting for the selected range.

Style name

Current formatting

197

4. If you want to drop any of the formatting that's applied to the selected range, uncheck any of the Style Includes check boxes.

5. Click OK. Excel creates the style.

Using a Style

The benefit of creating a style is that you can easily use the same set of formats over and over. To use a style, follow these steps:

1. Select the range that you want to format.

2. Select the Format Style command.

3. Click on the down arrow next to the Style Name list to see a list of style names.

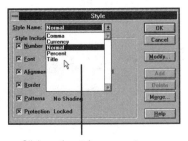

Click on the style you want.

4. Click on the style you want.

5. Click OK. Excel applies the style to the selected cell or range.

Creating a Style by Command

If you have not already formatted a range with the style you want, you can use the command method to create the style. Follow these steps:

1. Select the Format Style command. You see the Style dialog box.

2. Type the style name in the Style Name text box.

3. Click on the Add button.

4. Click on the Modify button. The Format Cells dialog box appears.

Click on the tab you want.

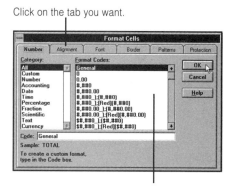

Select the options you want.

5. Click on the tab you want (Number, Alignment, Font, Border, Patterns, and Protection), and then select the appropriate options. For more information on these options, see the other chapters in this part.

6. Click OK, and Excel creates the style.

Deleting a Style

If you no longer need a style, you can delete it. To do so, follow these steps:

1. Select the Format Style command. You see the Style dialog box.

2. Display the Style Name drop-down list, and then click on the style you want to delete.

3. Click on the Delete button. Excel deletes the style. All cells formatted with the deleted style will revert to normal style.

Cheat Sheet

Using AutoFormat

1. Select Format AutoFormat.
2. From the Table Format list, click the format you want.
3. Click OK.

Customizing the AutoFormat

1. Select Format AutoFormat.
2. Click the Options button.
3. Check which format you want to apply.
4. Click OK.

30

Using AutoFormat

Use
AutoFormat
if data is
set up like
a Table

Many worksheets are set up like tables: a set of columns with headings, rows with headings, and summary information. If your worksheet is set up in this format, you can use the AutoFormat feature to quickly apply a set of attractive formats.

Basic Survival

Using AutoFormat

Excel provides over 15 different formats to choose from. The formats include preset number, border, font, pattern, alignment, column width, color, and row height selections. Here are some examples of the different formats:

- Simple
- Classic
- Colorful
- Accounting
- List
- 3D Effects

To use AutoFormat, follow these steps:

1. Select the Format AutoFormat command. You will see the AutoFormat dialog box.

Click on a
style here.

Preview the
style here.

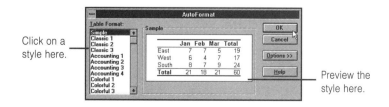

2. From the Table Format list, click on the format you want.

3. Click OK, and Excel applies the set of formatting. The following two figures show two different AutoFormat styles, Classic 1 and Colorful 3.

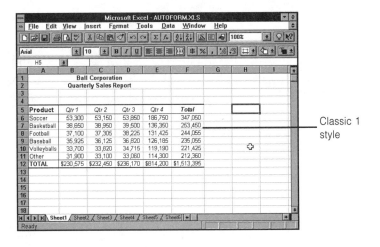

Classic 1 style

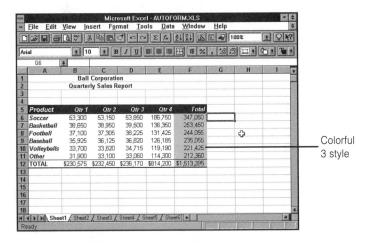

Colorful 3 style

Beyond Survival

Customizing the AutoFormat

If you want to use only a part of a particular format, you can customize the format, applying only the options you want. To do so, follow these steps:

1. Select the Format AutoFormat command. You will see the AutoFormat dialog box.

2. Click on the Options button.

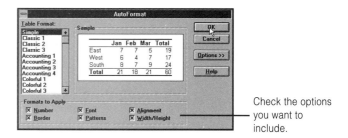

Check the options you want to include.

3. Check which formats you want to apply: Number, Border, Font, Patterns, Alignment, or Width/Height.

4. Click OK. Excel applies only the selected formats to the table.

Cheat Sheet

Setting Page Breaks

1. Select the cell where you want to insert the page break.
2. Select Insert Page Break.

Setting Margins

1. Select File Page Setup.
2. Select the Margins tab.
3. Click the margin text box you want to change.
4. Delete and retype the entry.
5. To change the header or footer margin, click in the Header or Footer text box.
6. Delete and retype the entry.
7. Click OK.

Setting Up the Page

1. Select File Page Setup.
2. Select the Page tab.
3. Select the options you want.
4. Click OK.

Setting Up the Sheet

1. Select File Page Setup.
2. Click the Sheet tab.
3. Select the options you want.
4. Click OK.

31

Setting Up the Page

Getting your worksheet to print just right may require some adjustments. The Page Setup options enable you to enter new margins, control the direction in which the worksheet is printed, size the worksheet on one page, and set other options. The Page Setup dialog box includes four tabs: Page, Sheet, Margins, and Header/Footer. This chapter covers the first three tabs. For information on headers and footers, see the next chapter.

Basic Survival

Setting Page Breaks

Excel will enter page breaks automatically based on the page setup options you have selected (margins, scaling, and so on). If needed, you can force a page break. For example, suppose that your worksheet contains sales summary information for each division in your company, and you want each division summary to print on a separate page. You can enter manual page breaks to achieve the result you want.

1. Select the cell where you want to insert the page break. The page break will be inserted above the selected cell.

2. Select the Insert Page Break command. A dotted line appears on-screen, indicating the page break.

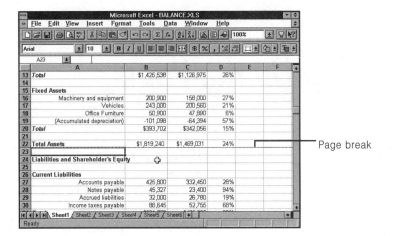

To remove a page break, select the cell immediately below the page break, and select the Remove Page Break command from the Insert menu.

Make sure the selected cell is in the first column if you only want a horizontal page break. If you select a cell that's not in column A and insert a page break, Excel will break the worksheet into quadrants.

Setting Margins

By default, Excel creates a 1-inch top and bottom margin and a .75-inch left and right margin. Headers and footers have a .5-inch margin. You can change these settings by following these steps:

1. Select the File Page Setup command.

2. Select the Margins tab. You will see the Margins tab of the Page Setup dialog box.

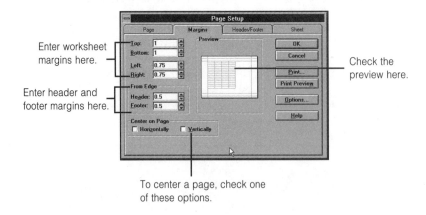

3. Click in the margin text box you want to change: Top, Bottom, Left, or Right.

4. Delete and retype the entry, or edit the existing entry.

5. If you want to change the header or footer margin, click in the Header or Footer text box in the From Edge area.

6. Delete and retype the entry, or edit the existing entry.

7. If you can't get your printout to look right on the page, try centering it. Select the Horizontally check box to center the page horizontally (across). Select the Vertically check box to center the page vertically (up and down).

8. Click OK, and Excel makes the changes. You won't notice the changes in the worksheet, but you can preview the worksheet to see how it will look when printed. The following figure shows a preview. For information on previewing a worksheet, see Chapter 33, "Previewing a Worksheet."

Two-inch top margin

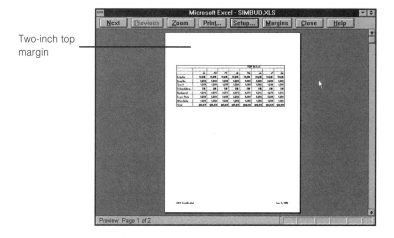

Beyond Survival

Setting Up the Page

Options for setting up the page include orientation, scaling, and page numbering. Using the Page Setup dialog box, you can adjust these options to suit your needs.

Lots of
columns =
landscape
orientation

Orientation refers to the direction in which data is printed on the page. *Portrait orientation* prints a worksheet across the short edge of the page. If your worksheet has many columns, you might want to switch to *landscape orientation*, in which the data is printed across the long side of the page.

Scaling is the process of changing the size of an object without changing its dimensions. For example, a one-page worksheet that includes all the information you need is probably ideal. However, some worksheets might be a little bit too big or too small to fit on one page. You can adjust a worksheet to fill one page in either of these ways:

- If you want to scale the worksheet a percentage, select the Adjust to option and enter a percentage to scale. For instance, you might scale the worksheet by 70%. You might need to experiment with the value to get the worksheet to fit just right. (You can also scale the other way—enter a number larger than 100—to enlarge the worksheet.)

- If you don't want to worry about guessing the percentage rate, you can select the Fit to page option and enter the dimensions of the page (1 by 1, for instance). Excel will fit the worksheet within those specifications.

Follow these steps to set page options:

1. Select the File Page Setup command.

2. Select the Page tab. You will see the Page tab of the Page Setup dialog box.

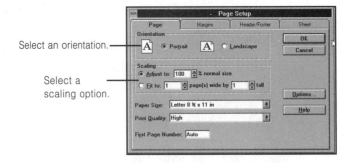

Select an orientation.

Select a
scaling option.

3. Click on an orientation: Portrait or Landscape.

4. If you want to scale the page, click on the Adjust to option and enter a percentage to scale. Or, click on the Fit to page option and enter the dimensions of the pages (1 by 1, for instance).

5. If you want to change the paper size, display the Paper Size drop-down list and select the size you want.

6. If you want to change the print quality, display the Print Quality drop-down list and select the quality you want.

7. If you want to start numbering pages with a different number, enter the number you want to use in the First Page Number text box.

8. Click OK. You won't notice any changes on-screen; to see the changes, you'll have to preview the worksheet. The following figure shows a preview of a worksheet in landscape orientation. (The worksheet in the figure has been scaled so that it fits on one page.) For information on previewing a worksheet, see Chapter 33, "Previewing a Worksheet."

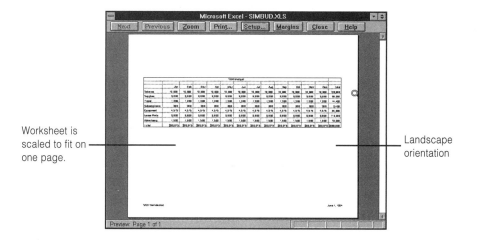

Worksheet is scaled to fit on one page.

Landscape orientation

Setting Up the Sheet

Turn off gridlines— They won't print

Sheet options control which elements of the worksheet (such as gridlines, notes, row headings, and so on) will be printed. You might want to make some changes based on your personal preferences. For example, if you don't like the clutter of all the gridlines, you can turn off gridlines.

Another common change is to repeat column or row headings on a multi-page worksheet. On worksheets that span two pages, the information on the second page might not make sense without proper headings. Suppose your two-page sales worksheet lists the product name in the first column. If the second page doesn't show the product names, it will be hard to tell what the numbers mean.

The following figure shows a preview of the second page of a two-page worksheet, without row and columns repeated. You can correct this problem by repeating columns or rows. For worksheets with many columns, you can repeat the column headings on all pages. For worksheets with many rows, you can repeat the row headings on all pages.

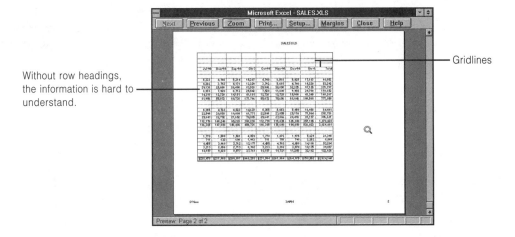

Without row headings, the information is hard to understand.

Gridlines

Follow these steps to set up the sheet.

1. Select the File Page Setup command.

2. Click on the Sheet tab. You will see the Sheet tab of the Page Setup dialog box.

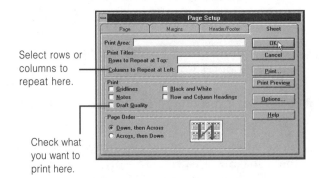

Select rows or columns to repeat here.

Check what you want to print here.

3. If you want to print just a range, enter the range in the Print Area text box.

4. If you want to print titles, click in the Rows to Repeat at Top and/or the Columns to Repeat at Left text boxes. Then click on the worksheet row or column you want to repeat. Excel enters a row or column reference (for instance, $A:$A indicates that column A will be repeated).

5. Check which elements to print: Gridlines, Notes, Draft Quality, Black and White, Row and Column Headings.

6. Click on a page order: Down, then Across or Across, then Down.

7. Click OK. To see the changes, preview the worksheet. The following figure shows a preview of the second page of a two-page worksheet. For information on previewing a worksheet, see Chapter 33, "Previewing a Worksheet."

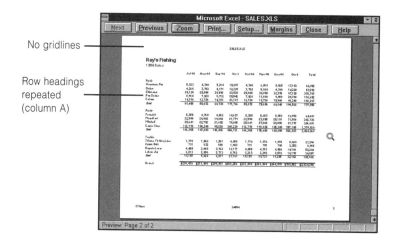

No gridlines ⎯

Row headings
repeated
(column A) ⎯

Cheat Sheet

Using a Predefined Header or Footer

1. Select File Page Setup.
2. Click the Header/Footer tab.
3. Click the down arrow next to the Header drop-down list box, and then select a format.
4. Click the down arrow next to the Footer drop-down list box, and then select a format.
5. Click OK.

Turning Off a Header or Footer

1. Click the down arrow next to the Header or Footer drop-down list.
2. Click none.

Creating a Custom Header or Footer

1. Select File Page Setup.
2. Click the Header/Footer tab.
3. Click the Custom Header or Custom Footer button.
4. Move to the section in which you want to enter text.
5. Enter the codes you want.
6. Click OK.

32

Adding Headers and Footers

Worksheet titles, revision dates, company names, page numbers, and file names are just a few of the types of information you can include in a header or footer. Information in a *header* is printed at the top of each page in the worksheet. Information in a *footer* is printed at the bottom of each page. You can use the default headers and footers, select a predefined header or footer, or create your own.

Basic Survival

Using a Predefined Header or Footer

When you print a worksheet, you might be surprised to see information at the top and bottom. That's because Excel uses a predefined header and footer automatically. By default, Excel prints the worksheet name in the header and the page number in the footer. Headers are printed one-half inch from the top of the page, and footers are printed one-half inch from the bottom. You can change these margins, if you want. (See Chapter 31, "Setting Up the Page.")

Excel provides some predefined headers and footers that combine different information. Check these before you go to the trouble of creating your own custom header. Note that Excel will use your name, your company name, the actual page number, the sheet name, the current date, and the workbook name assigned. The predefined headers and footers are listed below.

- *Your name*, *page number*, *current date* (Example: Shelley O'Hara, Page 1, 4/4/94)

- Prepared by *your name*, *date*, *page number* (Example: Prepared by Shelley O'Hara, 4/4/94, Page 1)

- *Your company name* Confidential, *sheet name*, *page number* (Example: SKO Confidential, Sales Forecast, Page 1)

- *Page number*

- *Sheet name* (Example: Sales Forecast)

- *Sheet name*, *page number* (Example: Sales Forecast, Page 1)

- Page 1 of *?* (Example: Page 1 of 12)

- *Company name* Confidential, *date*, *page number* (Example: SKO Confidential, 4/4/94, Page 1)

- *Workbook name* (Example: DIVSALES.XLS)

- *Workbook name*, *page number* (Example: DIVSALES.XLS, Page 1)

- *Sheet name*, *company name* Confidential, *page number* (Example: Sales Forecast, SKO Confidential, Page 1)

- *Company name* Confidential, *current date*, *page number* (Example: SKO Confidential, 4/4/94, Page 1)

To use a predefined header or footer, follow these steps:

1. Select the File Page Setup command.

2. Click on the Header/Footer tab. You will see the Header/Footer tab of the Page Setup dialog box.

Preview the header here.

Click on a header style.

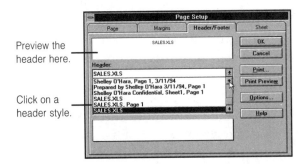

3. To use a predefined header, click on the down arrow next to the Header drop-down list box; then click on one of the predefined formats. Excel displays a preview of the header in the dialog box.

4. To use a predefined footer, click on the down arrow next to the Footer drop-down list box; then click on a predefined footer. Excel displays a preview of the footer in the dialog box.

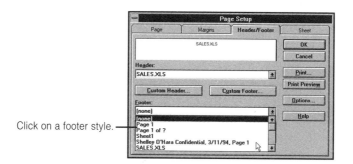

Click on a footer style.

Preview The worksheeT To see The header or footer

5. Click OK. In the worksheet, the headers and footers aren't displayed. To see them, you have to preview the worksheet. The following figure shows a preview. For information on previewing a worksheet, see Chapter 33, "Previewing a Worksheet."

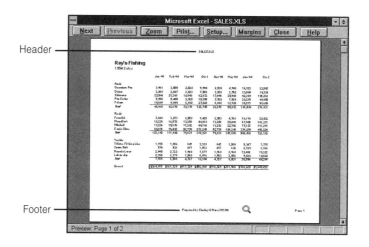

Header

Footer

Turning Off a Header or Footer

None = no header or footer

If you don't want to use a header or footer, display the Header/Footer tab. Then click on the down arrow next to the Header drop-down list or the Footer drop-down list and click on none.

Beyond Survival

Creating a Custom Header or Footer

If none of the predefined headers or footers is what you need, you can create your own. Excel provides some buttons that enable you to quickly insert the page number, date, and so on. To create a custom header or footer, follow these steps:

1. Select the File Page Setup command.

2. Click on the Header/Footer tab. You will see the Header/Footer tab of the Page Setup dialog box.

3. Click on the Custom Header button to create a customized header.

4. Move to the section in which you want to enter text. You can enter text in the Left Section, Center Section, and Right Section of the header or footer.

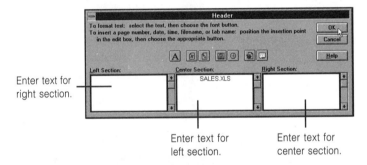

Enter text for right section.

Enter text for left section.

Enter text for center section.

5. Enter the text and codes you want. To insert a code, click on the buttons that appear in the dialog box. Here's what each button does:

Button	Description
A	Changes the font.
#	Inserts the page number.
⊕	Inserts the number of pages (for instance, you can print **Page 1 of 12** using this button and the preceding button).
📅	Inserts the date.

Button	Description
⊕	Inserts the time.
⑤	Inserts the file name.
▣	Inserts the worksheet name.

6. Click OK to return to the Page Setup dialog box.

7. To create a custom footer, click on the Custom Footer button; then follow steps 4–6 to create the custom footer. The following figure shows a footer using the company name for the left section, the date for the center, and the number of pages for the right.

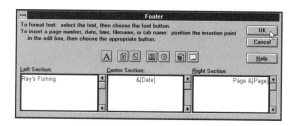

8. Click OK to close the Page Setup dialog box. You are returned to the worksheet. To view your custom header or footer, preview the page. For information on previewing a worksheet, see Chapter 33, "Previewing a Worksheet."

Custom footer —

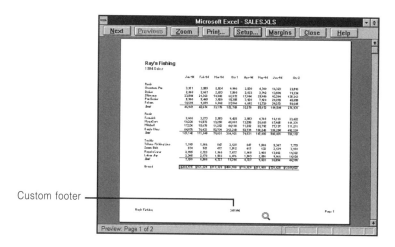

Cheat Sheet

Previewing a Worksheet

1. Select File Print Preview.

Changing the Margins in Print Preview

1. In print preview, click the Margins button.

2. Point to the margin guideline you want to change.

3. Drag the guideline to the new location.

Zooming the Preview

1. Move the magnifying glass mouse pointer over the area you want to preview.

2. Click the mouse button.

33

Previewing a Worksheet

Preview The worksheet before printing

Before you send a worksheet to the printer, you should check an on-screen version using Print Preview. In the print preview screen, you can tell how the overall worksheet will print. If it looks OK, you can print it. If you need to make changes, you can make them, preview the worksheet again, and then print.

Basic Survival

Previewing a Worksheet

It's difficult to see the overall look of the worksheet when you are viewing only a section of it. To see formatting changes, such as headers and footers and margin changes, and to get an overall sense of how the worksheet will look on the page, you need to preview it.

To preview the worksheet, follow these steps:

1. Select the File Print Preview command. Excel displays a preview.

Click here to display the next page.

Click here to print the worksheet.

Click here to return to regular view.

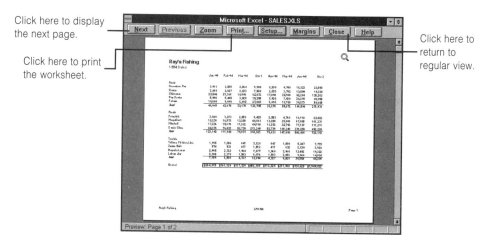

2. Click Close to return to the regular view.

As you look at the worksheet in print preview, check these elements:

- Does the worksheet fit on one page? Do you need to squeeze it onto one page?

- If the worksheet is longer than one page, do the page breaks occur at logical places? Or do you need to adjust the page breaks?

- If the worksheet is longer than one page, is the second page self-explanatory? Or do you need to repeat column or row headings?

- Overall, does the important information stand out? Do you need to add shading or borders to make the key information stand out?

- Is the worksheet too busy? Do you need to turn off gridlines or tone down some of the formatting?

- Is the information easy to read and follow? Do you need to add a worksheet title? Do you need to add explanatory text boxes?

- Do the margins work okay? Or do you need to adjust them?

- Are the headers and footers okay? Do they contain the information you want?

To view other pages in the worksheet, click on the Next or Previous buttons. To print the worksheet, click on the Print button.

Beyond Survival

Changing Margins in Print Preview

When you are in print preview, you can make changes to the worksheet. For example, click on the Setup button to display the Page Setup dialog box, and then make any changes. You can also change the margins while previewing. To do so, follow these steps:

1. In print preview, click on the Margins button. Excel displays guidelines for each of the margins.

2. Point to the margin guideline you want to change. When the mouse pointer is in the right spot, it changes to a line with two arrows.

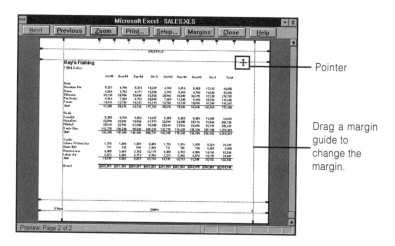

Pointer

Drag a margin guide to change the margin.

3. Drag the guideline to the new location. Excel changes the margin.

Zooming the Preview

The worksheet can be difficult to read in preview mode, so Excel gives you the option of zooming (enlarging) the worksheet if necessary. To zoom in on a particular spot, move the magnifying glass mouse pointer over the area you want to preview and click the mouse button, or click on the Zoom button. Excel zooms the preview.

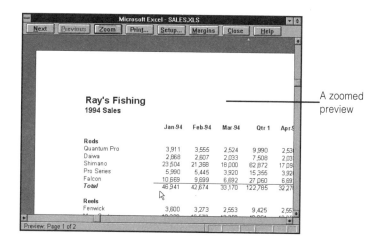

A zoomed preview

Cheat Sheet

Printing a Workbook

- Select File Print and click OK.

  OR

- Click the Print button 🖨.

Printing Part of a Workbook

1. Select File Print.
2. In the Print What area, select what you want to print.
3. In the Copies text box, type the number of copies.
4. In the Page Range area, select whether you want to print all pages or a range.
5. Click OK.

Selecting a Printer

1. Select File Print.
2. Click the Printer Setup button.
3. Click on the printer that you want to use from the Printer list.
4. Click OK.

Setting Printer Options

1. Select File Page Setup.
2. Click the Options button.
3. Make changes to any of the options.
4. Click OK.

34

Printing a Workbook

You will probably want to share the information you've been analyzing in Excel with someone else. You will want to print it, possibly to review a hard copy or to distribute it to others. Excel offers many printing features. You can select how many copies are printed, what is printed, and which printer is used.

Basic Survival

Printing a Workbook

Before you print, you need to set up the page correctly, as described in Chapter 31, "Setting Up the Page," and Chapter 32, "Adding Headers and Footers." It's also a good idea to preview the printout to be sure it looks the way you want it to, as described in Chapter 33, "Previewing a Worksheet." After everything is set up, you can print. If you want to print the active worksheet without selecting any options, just click the Print button. Excel will send your worksheet to the printer, without showing you the Print dialog box.

To print the entire worksheet, follow these steps:

1. Select the File Print command. The Print dialog box appears.

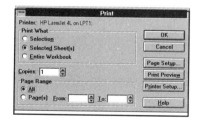

2. Click OK. Excel prints the worksheet.

Ray's Fishing 1994 Sales								
	Jan-94	Feb-94	Mar-94	Qtr 1	Apr-94	May-94	Jun-94	Qtr 2
Rods								
Quantum Pro	3,911	3,555	2,524	9,990	2,530	4,740	16,323	23,593
Daiwa	2,868	2,607	2,033	7,508	2,033	3,792	13,509	19,334
Shimano	23,504	21,368	18,000	62,872	17,094	25,900	92,269	135,263
Pro Series	5,990	5,445	3,920	15,355	3,920	7,920	28,215	40,055
Falcon	10,669	9,699	6,692	27,060	6,692	12,720	39,273	58,685
Total	46,941	42,674	33,170	122,785	32,270	55,072	189,589	276,931
Reels								
Fenwick	3,600	3,273	2,553	9,425	2,553	4,760	16,110	23,422
MegaCast	18,230	16,573	13,258	48,061	13,258	20,088	67,985	101,331
Mitchell	17,236	15,670	11,282	44,188	11,282	22,792	77,137	111,211
Eagle Claw	84,076	76,433	52,739	213,248	52,739	100,240	339,250	492,229
Total	123,142	111,948	79,831	314,921	79,831	147,880	500,481	728,193
Tackle								
Trilene Fishing Line	1,195	1,086	847	3,128	847	1,580	5,347	7,775
Zoom Bait	574	521	417	1,512	417	632	2,139	3,188
Rapala Lures	2,995	2,723	1,960	7,677	1,960	3,960	13,402	19,322
Lakco Jigs	2,395	2,178	1,503	6,076	1,503	2,856	9,666	14,024
Total	7,159	6,508	4,727	18,394	4,727	9,028	30,554	44,309
Grand	$264,975	$161,129	$117,729	$456,100	$116,829	$211,980	$720,625	$1,049,433

Ctrl + P = Print

If the worksheet doesn't print, be sure that the printer is turned on and is on-line. Also, be sure you've installed the printer correctly through Windows (see your printer or Windows manual).

To print more than one worksheet, see Chapter 41, "Using Find File."

Beyond Survival

Printing Part of a Worksheet

By default, Excel prints all the selected sheets. If you want, you can print only part of a worksheet or you can print all worksheets in a workbook. You can also print a range of pages. Follow these steps to change what is printed:

1. Select the File Print command. You see the Print dialog box.

2. In the Print What area, select what you want to print: Selection, Selected Sheet(s), or Entire Workbook.

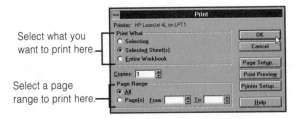

Select what you want to print here.

Select a page range to print here.

3. In the Copies text box, type the number of copies you want printed.

4. In the Page Range area, select whether you want to print all pages or a range. If you specify a range, enter the starting and ending page numbers in the From and To text boxes.

5. Click OK. Excel prints the worksheet(s).

Selecting a Printer

Excel will use the printer that is selected through the Windows Control Panel. If that is the only printer you use, you won't have to worry about selecting a printer. However, if you have access to more than one printer, you can select which printer to use. For instance, in some offices or homes, there might be two printers available. Or you may have a printer and a fax modem. If so, you can switch to the printer you want by following these steps:

1. Select the File Print command to access the Print dialog box.

2. Click on the Printer Setup button. You see the Printer Setup dialog box. This dialog box lists the printers you have installed through Windows.

Click on the printer you want.

3. Click on the printer that you want to use from the Printer list.

4. Click OK. The next time you print, Excel will print to the selected printer.

Setting Printer Options

In addition to being able to control the printer, you can also control certain printer settings such as the paper size, the number of copies, and other options. (The available options will vary, depending on the type of printer you have.) To change the printer options, follow these steps:

1. Select the File Page Setup command. The Page Setup dialog box appears.

2. Click on the Options button. You see the Setup dialog box for your printer.

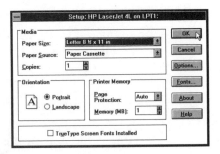

3. Make changes to any of the options. (The options will vary depending on what type of printer you have.) Common options include Paper Size, Paper Source, Orientation, Copies, and Graphics Resolution.

4. Click OK. Excel updates the printer setup.

PART 4

Timesavers

Excel includes a number of features that can save you time and make your work more efficient. Excel also includes features you can use to check your worksheet: check the spelling, check the formulas, and more. This part focuses on timesaving features and includes the following topics:

- Inserting Cells, Columns, and Rows
- Deleting Cells, Rows, and Columns
- Finding and Replacing Data
- Creating a Custom List
- Using Names
- Checking Spelling
- Using Find File

Cheat Sheet

Inserting Cells

1. Select the cell where you want to insert a new cell.
2. Select Insert Cells.
3. Click an option.
4. Click OK.

Inserting Rows and Columns

1. Select the row or column where you want to insert the new row or column.
2. Select Insert Rows or Insert Columns.

35

Inserting Cells, Columns, and Rows

If you created a worksheet on paper and forgot a key value in the middle, you'd have to erase an entry to make room and then reenter all the following values. Not so with Excel. With Excel, you can easily insert cells, rows, and columns if you leave something out or need to add something later.

Basic Survival

Inserting Cells

Suppose that you need to insert some information right in the middle of existing information. What's the best way to do this? Use the Insert Cells command by following these steps:

1. Select the cell where you want to insert a new cell. If you want to insert several cells, select the number of cells equal to the number you want to add.

2. Select the Insert Cells command. You see the Insert dialog box.

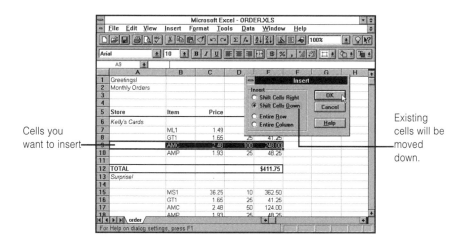

Cells you want to insert

Existing cells will be moved down.

3. Click on one of the following:

Shift Cells Right	Shifts existing cells to the right and inserts one cell.
Shift Cells Down	Shifts existing cells down and inserts one cell.
Entire Row	Shifts all cells in that row down and inserts a new row.
Entire Column	Shifts all cells in that column to the right and inserts a new column.

4. Click OK. Excel inserts the cell(s) and moves existing data in the specified direction.

New cells

Other cells
are moved
down.

You can move and insert and copy and insert at the same time. See Chapter 16, "Moving Data," and Chapter 17, "Copying Data."

Beyond Survival

Inserting Rows

A common worksheet editing change is to insert rows or columns. If you forget a category in your budget, for instance, you can insert a new row. Excel will move existing rows down to make room. Follow these steps:

1. Select the row where you want to insert the new row. The new row will be inserted above this row. If you want to insert several rows, select the number of rows equal to the number you want to insert.

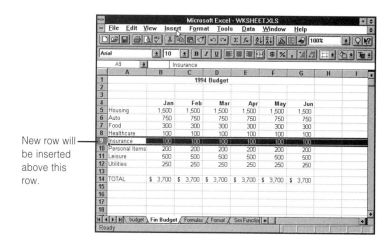

New row will be inserted above this row.

2. Select the Insert Rows command. Excel inserts the row and moves existing rows down.

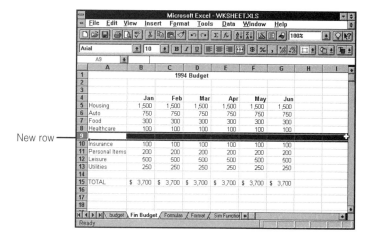

New row

When you insert a row or column, the new row or column does not include any formatting you may have applied to the surrounding rows or columns. You'll need to format this row or column.

Inserting Columns

Just as you can insert a row, you can easily insert a column. For example, you may want to add a column to a budget database that tracks actual spending and then calculates the variance. To insert a column, follow these steps:

1. Select the column where you want to insert the new column. The new column will be inserted to the left of this column. If you want

231

to insert several columns, select the number of columns equal to the number you want to insert.

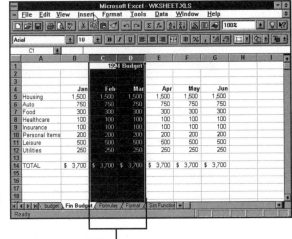

Two new columns will be inserted to the left of column C.

Ctrl + plus sign = Insert command.

2. Select the Insert Columns command. Excel inserts the column(s) and moves existing columns over.

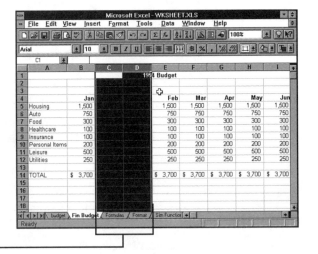

New columns

To delete a row or column, see the next chapter.

Cheat Sheet

Deleting Cells

1. Select the cell or range to delete.
2. Select Edit Delete.
3. Click Shift Cells Up or Shift Cells Left.
4. Click OK.

Deleting Rows and Columns

1. Select the row(s) or column(s) you want to delete.
2. Select Edit Delete.

Deleting Cells, Rows, and Columns

If you created a worksheet on paper and then wanted to delete an entry, you'd have to erase it and move all the others up. Not so with Excel. You can easily delete cells, rows, or columns.

When you delete a cell, row, or column, all data in that cell, row, or column will be deleted. Be sure to check the entire row or column before you delete it. In the on-screen area, the row or column may be blank, but there might be data off-screen in that row or column.

Also, after you delete the row or column, worksheet formulas that reference cells in the deleted row or column will display **#REF**. You need to change the formulas to refer to existing cells.

Basic Survival

Deleting Cells

Suppose that you have entered data in the middle of a worksheet and then decide you don't want that data. You don't want to delete just the contents, because that will leave a hole in the middle of the worksheet. You want to delete both the contents and the cells so that existing data moves up to fill in the blank cells. To do so, follow these steps:

1. Select the cell or range you want to delete.

2. Select the Edit Delete command. The Delete dialog box appears.

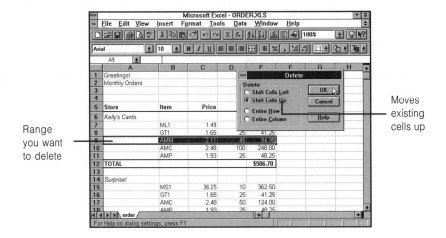

Range you want to delete

Moves existing cells up

3. Click on **Shift Cells Up** or **Shift Cells Left** to tell Excel how to shift existing data.

4. Click **OK**. Excel deletes the cells and the contents and moves existing data up.

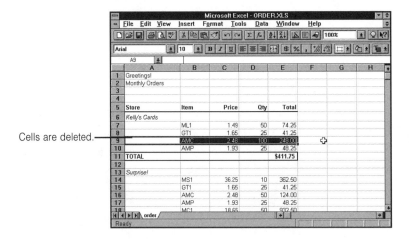

Cells are deleted.

If you want to delete the contents of the range, select the range and then select the **Edit Clear** command. The cells remain.

Beyond Survival

Deleting Columns   If you include a column in your worksheet that you no longer need, you can delete it. Keep in mind that not only do you delete the column and move all existing columns over, but you also delete any data in that column. To delete a column, follow these steps:

1. Select the column or columns you want to delete.

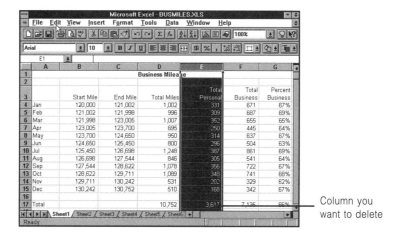

Column you want to delete

2. Select the Edit Delete command, and Excel deletes the column.

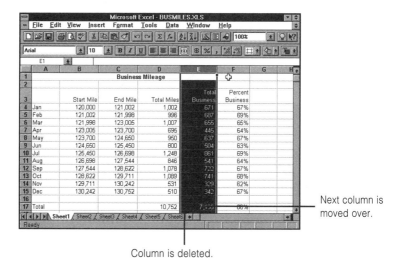

Next column is moved over.

Column is deleted.

Deleting Rows

Just as you can delete columns, you can delete rows you no longer need. Follow these steps:

Edit Undo
To undo a
deletion

1. Select the row or rows you want to delete.

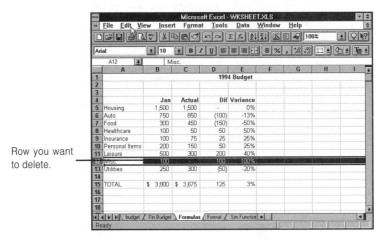

Row you want
to delete.

Ctrl + – To
Delete

2. Select the Edit Delete command. Excel deletes the row and all its data and moves existing rows up.

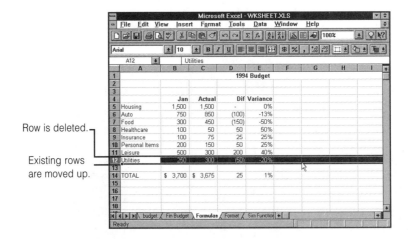

Row is deleted.

Existing rows
are moved up.

Cheat Sheet

Finding Data

1. Select Edit Find.
2. In the Find What text box, type the information you want to find.
3. Select the options you want.
4. Click on the Find Next button to find the first matching entry.
5. Click Find Next until you find the entry you want.
6. Click Close.

Replacing Data

1. Select Edit Replace.
2. Select the options you want.
3. Click the Find Next button to find the first matching entry.
4. Replace the text or skip to the next occurrence.
5. When all the replacements are made, click Close.

37

Finding and Replacing Data

A quick way to move to a certain part of a worksheet is to search for a word or phrase using the Find command. Then you can quickly edit that word or phrase, if necessary. A companion to the Find command is the Replace command. If you make a mistake when entering a value, with this command, you can search for and replace that value with the correct value.

Basic Survival

Finding Data

To find information quickly, you can use the Find command. This command searches through the values, formulas, or notes in your worksheet to find the specified text. For instance, suppose that you want to check a key value you used in a formula. You can search formulas for that entry. To search for data in the worksheet, follow these steps:

1. Select the Edit Find command. You will see the Find dialog box.

2. In the Find What text box, type the information you want to find.

Type the entry you want to find.

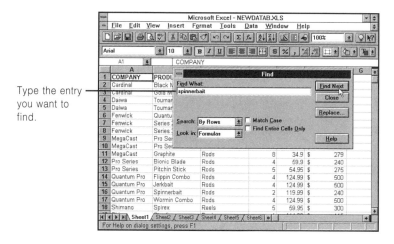

3. Choose from the following options:

- Tell Excel how to search by displaying the Search drop-down list and choosing By Rows or By Columns.

- Tell Excel where to look by displaying the Look in drop-down list and clicking on Formulas, Values, or Notes.

- If you want Excel to match the case as you've typed it, check the Match Case check box.

- If you want to find only entire entries (not partial entries), check the Find Entire Cells Only check box.

4. Click on the Find Next button to find the first matching entry.

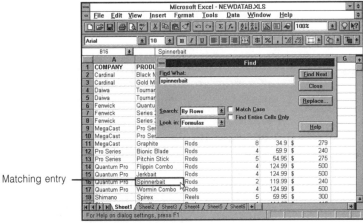

Matching entry

CTrl ＋ F =
Find

ShiＥT ＋ F4 =
Find NeXT

CTrl ＋
ShiＥT ＋ F4 =
Find
Previous

5. Continue clicking on Find Next until you find the entry you want. Then click Close to close the dialog box.

If Excel doesn't find a match, you will see a message saying so. Try the command again and double-check your spelling. Another reason Excel might not be able to find what you are looking for is that you are looking in the wrong entries. Remember that you tell Excel whether to look in formulas, values, or notes. Be sure the correct option is chosen.

Beyond Survival

Replacing Data

Suppose that you entered a company name (Pro Series, for example) throughout a worksheet, and then the company changed its name. With Excel, you don't have to scan every page looking for Pro Series and then make the change. You can make the change automatically.

Important!

Keep in mind that you can only search and replace values. You can't search and replace information in notes or in formulas.

To replace data, follow these steps:

1. Select the Edit Replace command. You will see the Replace dialog box.

2. In the Find What text box, type the information you want to find.

Type the entry you want to find.

Type the entry you want to use as the replacement.

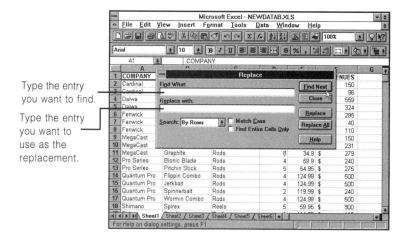

3. In the Replace with text box, type the entry you want to use as the replacement.

4. Choose from the following options:

- To change how Excel searches, display the Search drop-down list and click on By Rows or By Columns.

- If you want Excel to match the case as you've typed it, check the Match Case check box.

- If you want to find only entire entries (not partial entries), check the Find Entire Cells Only check box.

5. Click on the Find Next button to find the first matching entry. Excel moves to the first match (the Replace dialog box remains open).

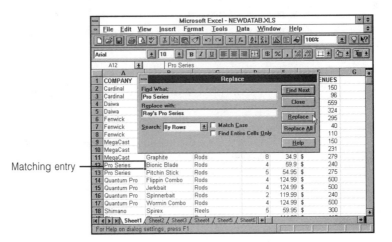

Matching entry

6. Perform one of the following operations:

- Click on Replace to replace this occurrence and move to the next.

- Click on Find Next to skip this occurrence and move to the next.

- Click on Replace All to replace all occurrences.

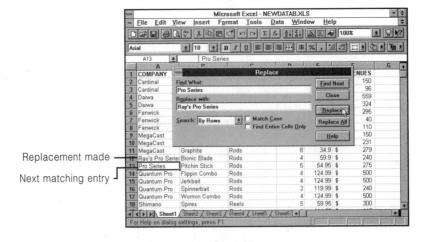

Replacement made

Next matching entry

7. When all the replacements are made, click Close to close the dialog box.

Ctrl + H = Replace

If Excel doesn't find a match, you will see a message saying so. Try the command again and double-check your spelling.

Cheat Sheet

Creating a List

1. Select the list in the worksheet.
2. Select Tools Options.
3. Click the Custom Lists tab.
4. Click the Import button.
5. Click the Add button to add the selected list.

Inserting a List

1. Type the first item in the list.
2. Drag the fill handle to fill the range.

Editing the List

1. Select Tools Options.
2. Click the Custom Lists tab.
3. Click the list you want to edit.
4. Edit the list items in the List Entries text box.
5. Click the Add button to add this list.

Deleting the List

1. Select Tools Options.
2. Click the Custom Lists tab.
3. Click the list you want to delete.
4. Click the Delete button.

38

Creating a Custom List

As you learned in Chapter 18, "Filling Data," you can use Excel to quickly fill a list of numbers, dates, or text entries. You can customize this feature to enter any series you want. For instance, suppose that you enter the same text entries (a list of parts, a list of names, a list of events) over and over in different worksheets. To save time, you can create your own series, called a *custom list*. Once this list is created, you can enter the first value and use the Fill handle to fill in the other values.

Basic Survival

Creating a List

You can create a list from entries you have already typed, or you can type the list entries manually. To create a custom list, follow these steps:

1. If you've already typed the list in a worksheet, select it.

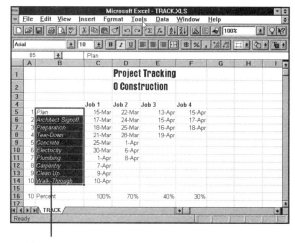

List you want to save

2. Select the Tools Options command.

3. Click on the Custom Lists tab. You will see the Custom Lists tab of the Options dialog box.

4. If you selected text in step 1, click on the Import button. Excel displays the list in the List Entries list in the dialog box. If you didn't select text for step 1, type the list items in the List Entries text box. Press Enter after each entry.

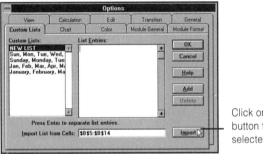

Click on this button to import a selected list.

5. When all the list items appear in the List Entries list, click on the Add button to add this list and keep the dialog box open. (You can then create other lists.) Or, click OK to add the list and close the dialog box.

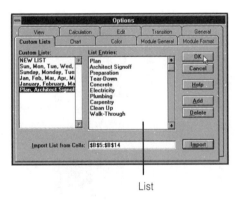

List

Inserting a List

You use regular fill techniques to fill the custom list into a range of worksheet cells. Follow these steps:

1. Type the first item in the list. When Excel fills the cells with the custom list entries, it will mimic the case of the first value you enter. For example, if you enter a list item in lowercase, Excel will fill the other values using lowercase.

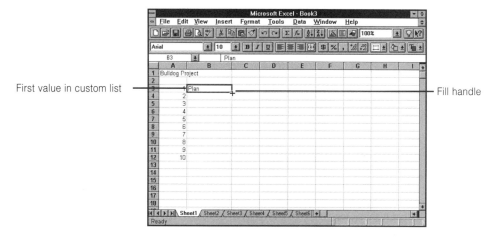

First value in custom list ——— Fill handle

Type The first entry and drag The fill handle

2. Drag the fill handle to fill the range with the custom list entries. Excel fills the range with your custom list. For more information on filling data, see Chapter 18, "Filling Data."

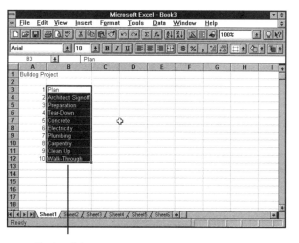

Custom list

Beyond Survival

Editing the List

If you need to change the list—delete entries, add entries, or edit the entries in the list—follow these steps:

1. Select the Tools Options command.

2. Click on the Custom Lists tab. You will see the Custom Lists tab of the Options dialog box.

3. In Custom Lists, click on the list you want to edit. Excel displays the list entries for the selected list.

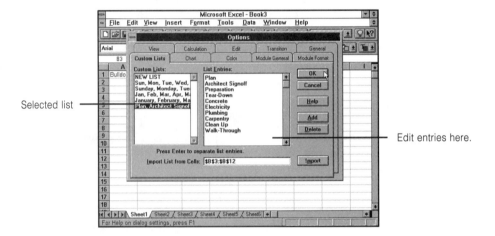

Selected list —

Edit entries here.

4. Edit the list items in the List Entries text box.

5. When you have finished editing the entries, click on the Add button to add this list and keep the dialog box open. (You can then create other lists.) Or, click OK to add the list and close the dialog box.

The next time you fill the custom list, Excel will use the edited list entries.

Deleting the List

If you no longer need a list, you can delete it from the Custom Lists tab. Follow these steps:

1. Select the Tools Options command.

2. Click on the Custom Lists tab.

3. Click on the list you want to delete.

4. Click on the Delete button. Excel removes the custom list from the tab.

Cheat Sheet

Creating a Name

1. Select the cell or range to name.
2. Select Insert Name Define.
3. Type the range name.
4. Click OK.

Using a Name in a Formula

1. Type an equal sign.
2. Click the arrow by the Name box to display a list of range names.
3. Click the name you want.

Moving to a Named Range

1. Select Edit Go To.
2. Click the range name.
3. Click OK.

Creating Names from Column Labels

1. Select both the range you want to name and the range that includes the headings.
2. Select Insert Name.
3. Select Create.
4. Click the row or column that contains that names you want to use.
5. Click OK.

39

Using Names

When you select a range, Excel uses the range coordinates to keep track of the range (for example, B6:B11 is a range). However, using range names makes it easier to create formulas and move to named ranges. For example, a formula that reads SALES–RETURNS is easier to understand than is B6:B11–G6:G11. Range names are easier to include in formulas, and it's much easier to remember a name like QTR1 than to remember the cell address that refers to that range.

Basic Survival

Creating a Name

You can name a single cell or a selected range in the worksheet. When you create a name and select that cell or range, Excel displays the range name in the Name box—next to the formula bar. Follow these steps to create a name:

1. Select the cell or range you want to name.

Range you want to name

2. Select the Insert Name command, and a submenu of choices appears.

3. Select the Define command. You will see the Define Name dialog box. Excel displays the range coordinates and suggests a name.

Suggested name ——

—— Range coordinates

4. Type the range name. (If you want to use the suggested name, skip to the next step.) When you name a range, begin the range name with a letter or underscore. You can use upper- and lower-case, and you can include up to 255 characters. Don't use a range name that looks like a cell reference, and don't include spaces.

5. Click OK. Excel names the range. When the range is selected, it appears in the Name box.

Range name ——

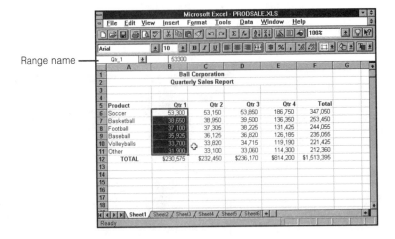

Ctrl + F3 =
Define Name
command

Using a Name in a Formula

After you name the range, you can easily insert it in a formula. To do so, follow these steps:

1. Type an equal sign (=) if you are creating a formula. If you want to insert a range name in an existing formula, double-click the cell that contains the formula, and then move the insertion point to where you want to insert the name.

2. Click on the arrow by the Name box to display a list of range names. You will see a drop-down list of names.

Click on the name you want to insert.

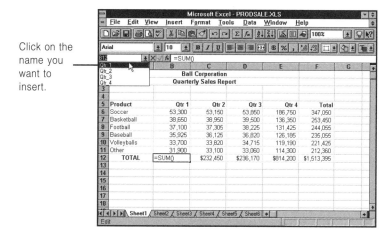

3. Click on the name you want. Excel inserts the range in the formula.

F3 = PasTe Name command

As an alternative to the steps above, you can type the equal sign, select the Insert Name Paste command, click on a name in the list, and then click OK.

Moving to a Named Range

Another benefit of naming ranges is that you can quickly go to a named range using the Go To command. Follow these steps:

1. Select the Edit Go To command. You will see the Go To dialog box.

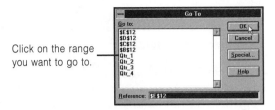

Click on the range
you want to go to.

2. Click on the range name in the list.

3. Click OK. Excel selects the named range.

Beyond Survival

**Creating Names
from Column
Labels**

If you want to name a range and you want to use column or row headings that are next to the range, you can create the names from the headings. Follow these steps:

1. Select both the range you want to name and the range that includes the headings. The headings and the named range must be next to each other.

2. Select the Insert Name command.

3. Select the Create command to access the Create Names dialog box.

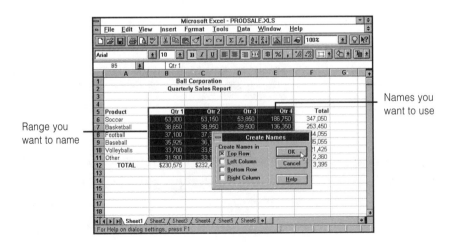

Range you
want to name

Names you
want to use

4. Click on whichever row or column contains the names you want to use: Top Row, Left Column, Bottom Row, or Right Column.

5. Click OK. Excel creates the range names.

Deleting a Name

If you name a range incorrectly or no longer want a range named, you can delete the range name. Simply follow these steps:

1. Select the Insert Name command.

2. Select the Define command. You see the Define Name dialog box.

3. Click on the range name you want to delete.

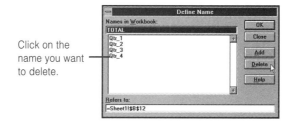

Click on the
name you want
to delete.

4. Click on the Delete button. If you are prompted, confirm the deletion.

5. Click OK, and Excel deletes the range name.

Pasting a List of Range Names

To keep track of which ranges you have named and what those names refer to, you can paste a list of range names in your worksheet. The resulting list will be two columns wide. The first column contains the range name, the second the range coordinates.

To paste a list of range names, follow these steps:

1. Select the first cell to contain the list.

2. Select the Insert Name Paste command. You will see the Paste Name dialog box.

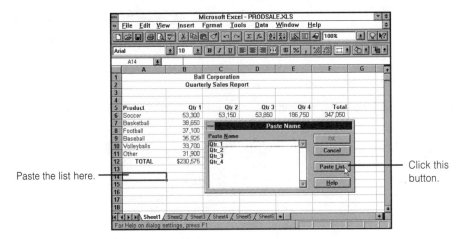

Paste the list here.

Click this button.

3. Click on the Paste List button. Excel pastes a list of range names.

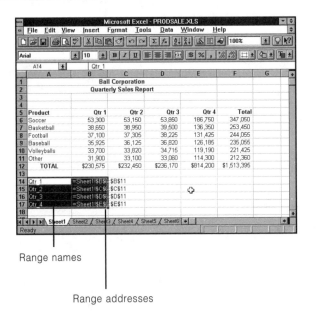

Range names

Range addresses

Cheat Sheet

Spell-Checking the Worksheet

1. Select a single cell.
2. Click the Spelling button.
3. Select options.
4. Correct each flagged word.
5. When a message appears telling you the spelling check is complete, click OK.

Creating a Custom Dictionary

1. Select Tools Spelling.
2. In the Add Words To text box, type a name for the dictionary.
3. Click the Add button.
4. Select Yes.
5. Type words in the Change To text box and click Add to add the words.
6. Click Cancel.

Specifying a Dictionary

1. Select Tools Spelling.
2. Click the down arrow next to the Add Words To drop-down list.
3. Click the dictionary you want to use.
4. Click Cancel.

Checking Spelling

Because you are concentrating on the figures rather than the words, it's easy to type an entry incorrectly when you are creating a worksheet. To make sure you don't have any spelling errors, you can check your spelling before you print your worksheet.

The spell check feature should not be a replacement for careful proof-reading of the worksheet. If the worksheet contains a lot of text, you should read the text carefully to make sure there aren't any mistakes. For instance, Excel doesn't know that you meant to type "two" when you actually typed "too." The spell check feature wouldn't catch that kind of error.

Proofread The Worksheet!

Basic Survival

Checking the Worksheet

If you want to check the entire worksheet, move to the first cell by pressing Ctrl+Home. (If you start in the middle, Excel checks from that point to the end of the worksheet and then asks whether you want to go to the top of the worksheet and check the rest.) If you want to check just a range, select the range first.

When you check the spelling, Excel compares the words in the worksheet to the words in its dictionary and flags any words it cannot find. Excel checks all values, hidden cells, text boxes, and buttons, but does not check formulas.

If no misspelled words are found, the Spelling dialog box never appears. A dialog box tells you that the document contains no misspelled words.

Excel flags words it thinks are misspelled. When a word is flagged, it doesn't necessarily mean it is misspelled. It just means Excel can't find the word in its dictionary. You can correct or ignore the flagged word.

To check the spelling in your worksheet, follow these steps:

1. Select a single cell to check the entire worksheet.

2. Select the Tools Spelling command or click on the Spelling button 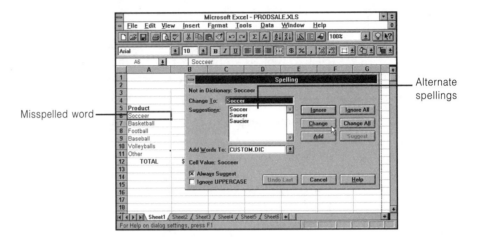.

Misspelled word ———

Alternate spellings

3. Do one of the following:

- If the word is misspelled and you see the correct spelling in the Suggestions list, click on the word. Excel lists the selected suggestion in the Change To text box. Click on Change to change just this occurrence of the misspelled word to the word in the Change To text box. Click on Change All to change all occurrences in this worksheet.

- If the word is misspelled, but the correct spelling is not listed, type the correct spelling in the Change To text box. Then click on Change to change just this occurrence of the misspelled word to the word in the Change To text box. Click on Change All to change all occurrences in this worksheet.

- If the word is spelled correctly, click on Ignore to ignore this word and continue. Click on Ignore All to ignore this word throughout the worksheet.

- If you use the word frequently, you can add it to the dictionary by clicking on the Add button. If you add it to the dictionary, Excel will not flag the word again.

4. Correct each flagged word.

5. When you see a message saying the spell check is complete, click OK.

Beyond Survival

Controlling the Spell Check

By default, Excel always suggests alternative spellings. If you'd prefer not to have these displayed, uncheck the Always Suggest check box in the Spelling dialog box.

Also by default, Excel flags uppercase words. If you want to skip uppercase words, check the Ignore UPPERCASE check box in the Spelling dialog box.

Uncheck this box if you don't want suggestions listed.

Check this box to skip uppercase words.

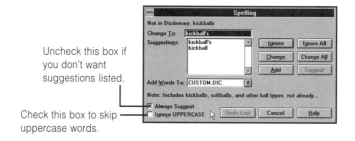

Creating a Custom Dictionary

When you add words to the dictionary, they are stored in the CUSTOM.DIC dictionary file. For most users, one custom dictionary will be plenty. If you want, though, you can create more than one dictionary and switch between them.

Once you've created the new dictionary, you can add words as you perform spell checks or you can type them in manually. You can start the speller and switch dictionaries at any time. To create a custom dictionary, follow these steps:

1. Select the Tools Spelling command.

2. In the Add Words To text box, type a name for the dictionary.

Name of new dictionary

3. Click on the Add button. You will be asked to confirm that you want to create a new dictionary.

4. Select Yes to confirm that you do want to create a new dictionary.

5. Type words in the Change To text box and click on Add to add words. Or, just add words as you do a spell check.

6. Click on Cancel to close the dialog box.

Specifying a Dictionary

When you have more than one custom dictionary, you can tell Excel which dictionary to use for a spell check. Follow these steps to specify a dictionary:

1. Select the Tools Spelling command.

2. Click on the down arrow next to the Add Words To drop-down list. You will see a list of custom dictionaries.

Click on the dictionary you want to use.

3. Click on the dictionary you want to use.

4. Click on Cancel to close the dialog box.

Cheat Sheet

Starting Find File

1. Select File Find File.
2. If the Search dialog box appears, enter the file name in the File Name box.
3. If you see the file you want, click on it.
4. Click OK.

Opening a Workbook

1. Start Find File and list your files.
2. Click the file you want to open.
3. Click the Open button.

Deleting a Workbook

1. Start Find File and display the workbook you want to delete.
2. Click the workbook you want to delete.
3. Click the Commands button.
4. Select Delete.
5. Click Yes.

Printing a Group of Files

1. Start Find File and display the files you want to print.
2. Select the files you want to print.
3. Click on the Commands button.
4. Click Print.

Copying a File

1. Start Find File and display the workbook you want to copy.
2. Click the workbook you want to copy.
3. Click the Commands button.
4. Select Copy.
5. Type a file name in the Path text box.
6. Choose a drive and directory.
7. Click OK.

41

Using Find File

In addition to all the worksheet, charting, database, and other tools provided with Excel, there is also a file manager program. You can use this feature to copy, delete, sort, open, and print files.

Basic Survival

Starting Find File

The first time you use the Find File feature, you are prompted to enter search criteria (tell Excel which files to list in which directories). After that, you aren't prompted for search criteria; Excel just lists the last set of files. To start Find File and enter search criteria, follow these steps:

1. Select the File Find File command.

2. Do one of the following:

• If you see the Search dialog box, skip to the next step.

• If you see the file list you want, skip the remaining steps.

• If the file list doesn't display the files you want, click on the Search button. You will see the Search dialog box.

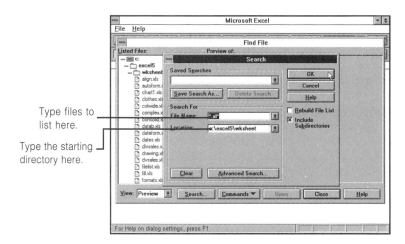

Type files to list here.

Type the starting directory here.

3. Enter what you want to find in the File Name box. You can type a single file name to locate one file, or you can use wild cards to display a set of files. For instance, to display all worksheet files, use the default entry *.xl*.

4. Type the path to search in the Location box. This is the starting directory. Excel will list matching files in this directory and all subdirectories if you check the Include Subdirectories check box.

5. Click OK. Excel displays a list of matching files.

File list ——

Preview ——

Opening a Workbook

Sometimes you know what a workbook contains, but you don't know the file name. If this happens, use Find File to display a preview of the file. When you find the file you want, you can open it directly from Find File. Follow these steps:

1. Start Find File and list your files. (See the preceding section for information on listing files.)

2. Click on the file you want to open.

3. Click on the Open button. Excel opens the document and closes Find File.

Changing the View

By default, Excel displays a preview of the selected worksheet. If you want, you can display summary information (entered when you saved the file) or file information (date, time, file size, and so on). To change what is displayed, follow these steps:

1. Start Find File and display the workbooks you want to view.

2. Click on the down arrow next to the View list. You see a list of view options.

3. Click on the view you want: Preview, File Info, or Summary. Excel displays the file in the selected view.

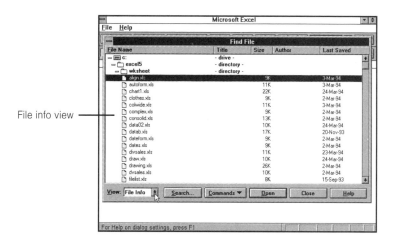

File info view

Deleting a Workbook

If you no longer need a file, you can delete it using Find File. Be sure you don't need the file, because without a special undelete program you will not be able to undo the deletion. To delete a file, follow these steps:

1. Start Find File and display the workbook you want to delete.

2. Click on the workbook you want to delete.

3. Click on the Commands button. You will see a pop-up list of commands.

4. Select the Delete command. Excel prompts you to confirm the deletion.

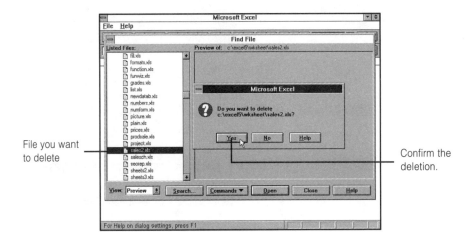

File you want
to delete

Confirm the
deletion.

5. Click on Yes. Excel deletes the file.

Beyond Survival

**Printing a Group
of Files**

If you have several worksheets to print, opening each file and then
selecting the Print command can be time consuming. Instead, print a
group of files using Find File. Follow these steps:

1. Start Find File and display the files you want to print. See the
section "Starting Find File" for information on selecting the
command and entering the search criteria.

2. Click on the first file you want to select. The file is highlighted.

3. Do one of the following:

- If the files are next to each other, point to the last file in the
group. Press and hold the Shift key and click the mouse
button. All files, including the first and last file, are selected.

- If the files are not next to each other, point to the next file
you want to select. Press and hold the Ctrl key and click on
the next file you want to select. Do this for each of the files
you want to select.

4. Click on the Commands button. You see a pop-up menu.

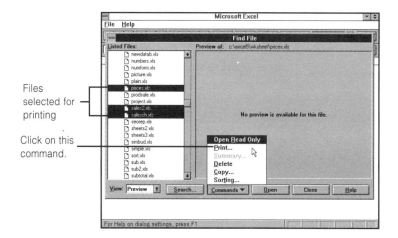

Files selected for printing

Click on this command.

5. Click on the Print command.

Copying a File

If you want to make an extra copy of a file or if you want to give a copy of a file to a coworker, you can use Find File to create the copy. Simply follow these steps:

1. Start Find File and display the workbook you want to copy.

2. Click on the workbook you want to copy.

3. Click on the Commands button.

4. Select the Copy command. The Copy dialog box appears.

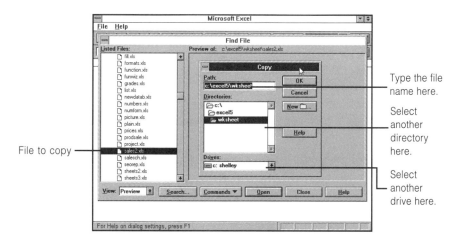

File to copy

Type the file name here.

Select another directory here.

Select another drive here.

271

5. Type a file name in the Path text box.

6. To save the file to another drive, display the Drives list and click on the drive you want.

7. To save the file to another directory, double-click on the directory name in the Directories list.

8. Click OK. Excel makes a copy of the file.

PART 5

Excel's Special Features

Excel is more than just a tool for working with numbers. With Excel, you can also create simple drawings using the drawing tools, turn your data into charts using the chart features, and keep track of data with the database features. This part focuses on these special features and includes the following topics:

- Using the Draw Tools
- Adding an Object
- Working with Objects
- Creating Charts
- Formatting Charts
- Creating Databases
- Working with Databases
- Creating Macros

Cheat Sheet

Using the Drawing Toolbar

1. Click the Drawing button.
2. Click a button from the palette.

Drawing an Object

1. Click the appropriate button in the Drawing toolbar.
2. Point to where you want the object to begin.
3. Drag across the worksheet to draw the object.
4. When the object is the right size, release the mouse button.
   (Optional) Add a pattern.
   (Optional) Add a drop shadow.

Drawing a Freeform Shape

1. Click on the Freeform or Filled Freeform button.
2. Click where you want the drawing to begin.
3. Drag to draw the first part of the shape.
4. Click where you want to end the first line and start a new line.
5. Drag to draw the second part.
6. Continue clicking and dragging until the object is finished.
7. Double-click the mouse button when you're finished.

Drawing Freehand

1. Click the Freehand button.
2. Drag across the worksheet.

Creating a Text Box

1. Click the Text Box button.
2. Drag across the worksheet to draw the text box.
3. Enter the text you want.

42

Using the Draw Tools

MusT have a
mouse To
draw!

Want to point out a key figure on a worksheet? Draw an arrow to it. Want to add some explanatory text? Add a text box. Excel provides drawing tools that you can use to create simple line drawings, like an arrow or a text box, that can really enhance a worksheet.

Basic Survival

Using the Drawing Toolbar

To draw on the worksheet, you first display the Drawing toolbar. Do so by clicking on the Drawing button on the Standard toolbar. Excel displays a palette of drawing buttons.

Button	Name	Description
	Line	Draws a line.
	Rectangle or square.	Draws a rectangle
	Ellipse circle.	Draws an ellipse or
	Arc	Draws an arc.
	Freeform shape.	Draws a freeform
	Text Box	Adds a text box.
	Arrow	Draws an arrow.
	Freehand	Draws a freehand shape.

continues

Button	Name	Description
	Filled Rectangle	Draws a filled rectangle or square.
	Filled Ellipse	Draws a filled ellipse or circle.
	Filled Arc	Draws a filled arc.
	Filled Freeform	Draws a freeform filled shape.
	Create Button	Draws a button on the worksheet.
	Drawing Selection	Enables you to select a drawing object.
	Bring To Front	Moves the selected object to the front—on top of other objects.
	Send To Back	Sends the selected object to the back—behind other objects.
	Group Objects	Groups individual objects into one object.
	Ungroup Objects	Ungroups objects.
	Reshape	Changes the shape of the object.
	Drop Shadow	Adds a shadow behind the object.
	Pattern	Fills the object with a pattern.

This chapter explains how to use the drawing buttons to create simple shapes. For information on editing an object, see Chapter 44, "Working with Objects."

Drawing a Line or Arrow

On a paper document, you can draw a line or an arrow to a key figure. You can do the same in an Excel worksheet. Follow these steps:

1. Click on the Line button or Arrow button .

2. Point to the spot on the worksheet where you want the line to begin. On-screen, you see a small cross.

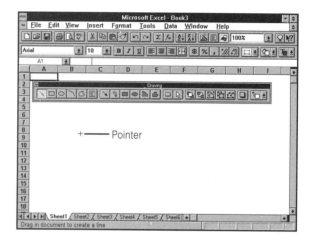

3. Hold down the mouse button and drag across the worksheet to draw the line.

4. When the line is the length you want, release the mouse button.

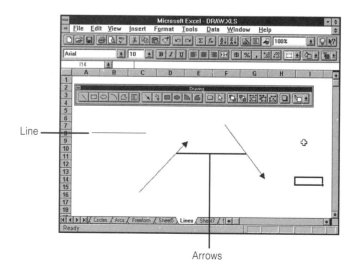

Line

Arrows

Drawing a Rectangle or Filled Rectangle

In addition to lines, you can draw rectangles. You can make them empty or filled with a color or pattern. You can also add a drop shadow to the object. To draw a rectangle or filled rectangle, follow these steps:

1. Click on the Rectangle button ▣ or the Filled Rectangle button ▣.

2. Point to the spot on the worksheet where you want the rectangle to begin.

Shift— draws a square

3. Hold down the mouse button and drag across the worksheet to what will be the rectangle's diagonally opposite corner. If you want to draw a perfect square, hold down the Shift key while dragging.

4. When the rectangle is the size you want, release the mouse button. The object remains selected.

5. If you want to change the pattern, click on the Pattern button ▣ and select a pattern and color. Note that this button works only when you draw a filled rectangle (if you selected the Filled Rectangle button in step 1). If you draw a regular rectangle, nothing happens. Also, you must click on a pattern first and then a color. If you just click on a color, without selecting a pattern, nothing happens.

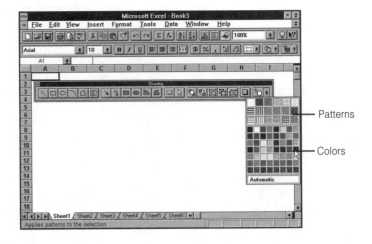

6. If you want to add a drop shadow, click on the Drop Shadow button 🔲.

The following figure shows examples of different rectangles.

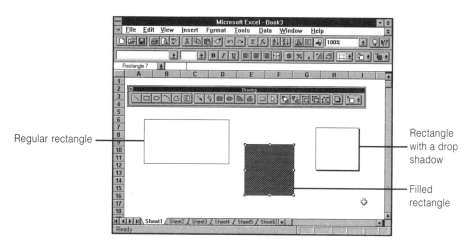

Regular rectangle —

Rectangle with a drop shadow

Filled rectangle

Drawing an Ellipse or Filled Ellipse

You can also draw an ellipse using the Drawing toolbar. To draw an ellipse or filled ellipse on your worksheet, follow these steps:

1. Click on the Ellipse button 🔘 or the Filled Ellipse button 🔘.

2. Point to the spot on the worksheet where you want the ellipse to begin.

3. Hold down the mouse button and drag across the worksheet to where you want the opposite side of the ellipse. If you want to draw a perfect circle, hold down the Shift key while dragging.

Shift—draws a perfect circle

4. When the ellipse is the size you want, release the mouse button. The object remains selected.

5. If you want to change the pattern, click on the Pattern button 🔲 and select a pattern and color. Note that this button works only when you draw a filled ellipse (if you selected the Filled Ellipse button in step 1). If you draw a regular ellipse, nothing

happens. Also, you must click on a pattern first and then a color. If you just click on a color, without selecting a pattern, nothing happens.

6. If you want to add a drop shadow, click on the Drop Shadow button ☐. The following figure shows examples of different ellipses.

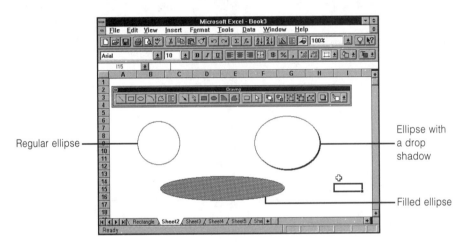

Regular ellipse —

Ellipse with a drop shadow

Filled ellipse

Drawing an Arc or Filled Arc

If you don't want to draw a complete circle or ellipse, you can use the Arc or Filled Arc buttons to draw part of a circle or ellipse. Follow these steps:

1. Click on the Arc button ☐ or the Filled Arc button ☐.

2. Point to the spot on the worksheet where you want the arc to begin.

3. Hold down the mouse button and drag across the worksheet to draw the arc.

4. When the arc is the size you want, release the mouse button. The object remains selected.

5. If you want to change the pattern, click on the Pattern button ☐ and select a pattern and color. Note that this button works only when you draw a filled arc (if you selected the Filled Arc button in step 1). If you draw a regular arc, nothing happens. Also, you must click on a pattern first and then a color. If you just click on a color, without selecting a pattern, nothing happens.

The following figure shows examples of different arcs.

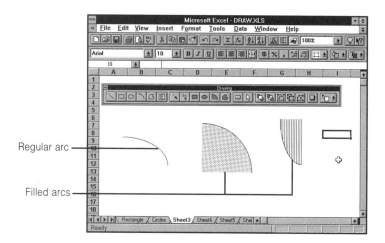

Regular arc

Filled arcs

Drawing a Freeform Shape

You can use the Line, Rectangle, and Ellipse tools to create simple shapes. But what if you want to draw a triangle or other shape? To draw polygon shapes, use the Freeform button by following these steps:

1. Click on the Freeform button or the Filled freeform button.

2. Click where you want the drawing to begin.

3. Drag to draw the first part of the shape.

4. Click when you want to end the first line and start a new line.

5. Drag to draw the second part.

6. Continue clicking and dragging to draw each side of the object.

7. When you are finished, double-click the mouse button.

The following figure shows examples of different freeform shapes.

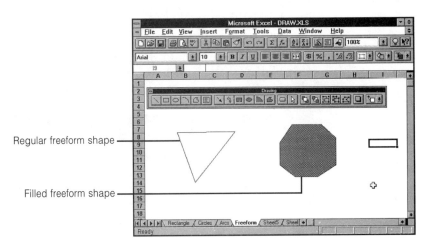

Regular freeform shape

Filled freeform shape

Drawing Freehand

Using the Freehand button is like drawing on-screen with an electronic pencil. To use this tool, follow these steps:

1. Click on the Freehand button ![freehand button].

2. Drag across the worksheet, just as if you were writing on the worksheet with a pen. Notice that the pointer looks like a small pencil.

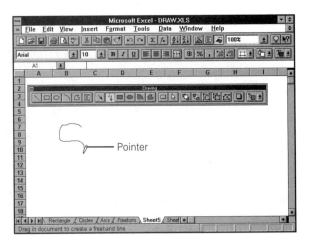

Pointer

Beyond Survival

Creating a Text Box

Adding a note to a worksheet can be difficult within the confines of the cell. You can wrap the text, but that expands the row height. You may wish that you could just add a Post-It note to the worksheet. Well, you can add a kind of Post-It note to the worksheet by adding a text box. A text box is a separate layer over the worksheet, so you can move and format the text box without affecting the data.

To create a text box, follow these steps:

1. Click on the Text Box button ▤.

2. Drag across the worksheet to draw the text box. The insertion point is inside the text box.

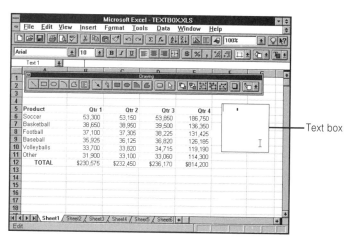

Text box

3. Type the text you want. You can use any of the editing and formatting tools that are available for worksheet data. For instance, you can make the text bold, change the alignment, and so on.

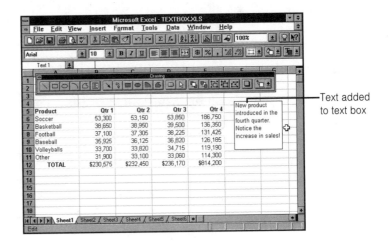

Text added
to text box

The text will wrap within the borders of the text box. You can resize the text box to change where the text wraps. See Chapter 44, "Working with Objects," for more information.

If you type more text than will fit, the text will scroll, but the size of the text box will remain unchanged. Either delete text so that it will fit or make the text box bigger.

You can add a pattern or drop shadow to the text box by clicking once on the text box to select it. Then click on the Pattern button and select a pattern or color, or click on the Drop Shadow button to add a drop shadow.

Cheat Sheet

Adding a Picture

1. Select Insert Picture.
2. Change to the appropriate directory.
3. Preview the picture by clicking the file name and then checking the Preview Picture check box.
4. Double-click the file name.

Adding an Object

1. Select Insert Object.
2. Click on the type of object to insert.
3. Create the object.
4. Return to the worksheet.

43

Adding an Object

You can create simple drawings using Excel's Drawing toolbar, as described in Chapter 42. But if you aren't a good artist even with Excel's Drawing toolbar, you can still add pictures to your worksheet. You can insert pictures you have created with Paintbrush (a Windows paint program), or you can insert clip-art files. Many applications (such as Word for Windows) come with several clip-art images, and you can purchase clip-art packages.

Basic Survival

Adding a Picture

To insert a picture, select a cell in the general area where you want to insert the picture. The picture is created as a separate layer, on top of the worksheet, so you won't overwrite data in any cells—even if you can move the picture after you insert it.

Follow these steps to add a picture:

1. Select the Insert Picture command. You see the Picture dialog box.

2. If necessary, change to the directory that contains the picture you want to insert. Excel lists the picture files in that directory.

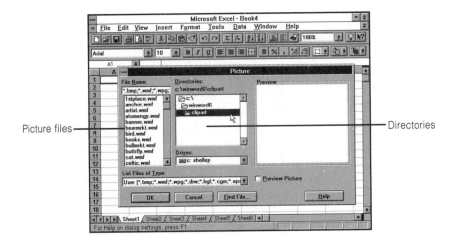

Picture files

Directories

Check Preview Picture To see a pre- view

3. To preview a picture, click once on the file name, and then check the Preview Picture check box.

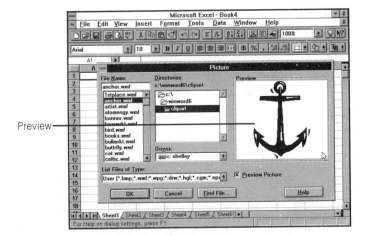

Preview

4. To insert the picture, double-click on the file name. Excel inserts the picture into the worksheet.

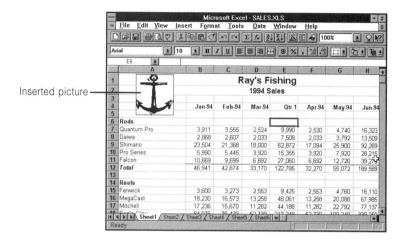

Inserted picture

For information on moving, deleting, and formatting the picture, see Chapter 44, "Working with Objects."

Beyond Survival

Adding an Object

You can embed other types of objects (for instance, a note, a WordArt object, or a Word for Windows document) into the worksheet. The example in this section covers how to insert a note. Follow these steps:

1. Select the Insert Object command. You see the Object dialog box.

2. If necessary, click on the Create New tab.

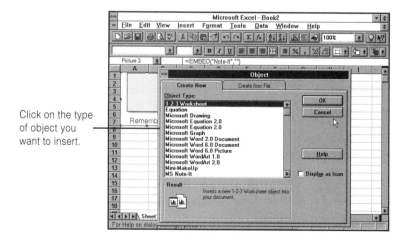

Click on the type of object you want to insert.

3. Click on the type of object to insert. For example, click on the MS Note-it option. Depending on what type of object you select, you will see a different dialog box or a different screen. For the MS Note-it, you see the Microsoft Note-it dialog box.

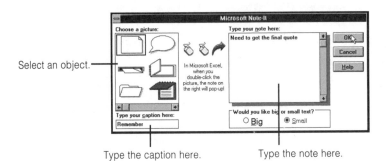

Select an object.

Type the caption here.   Type the note here.

4. Create the object. Again, depending on what type of object you are embedding, you follow different procedures. For the Note-it, select an icon for the note, type the caption for the note, and then type the note.

5. Return to the worksheet. If you are entering options in a dialog box, click OK. If you are working in a different screen, click back in the worksheet.

Excel embeds the object in the worksheet. You can double-click on the object to edit it, or (as in the case of the Note-it) to display the note.

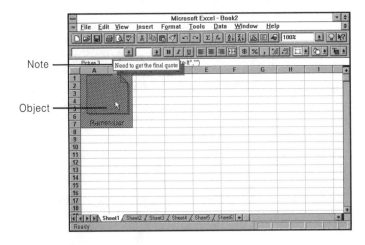

Note

Object

Cheat Sheet

Selecting an Object

- To select an object, click once on it.
- To select multiple objects, hold down Shift while clicking on the objects.

Moving an Object

1. Click on the object to select it.
2. Point to any border of the object and drag it to a new location.

Resizing an Object

1. Click once on the object to select it.
2. Point to one of the selection handles.
3. Drag the handle.
4. Release the mouse button when the object is the right size.

Formatting an Object

1. Double-click the object.
2. Click the Patterns tab.
3. Select the options you want.
4. Click OK.

44

Working with Objects

In an Excel worksheet, you can draw objects, add pictures, or create charts. Each of these items is created as a separate layer over the worksheet and is generically called an *object*. Because the object is a separate layer over the worksheet, you have a great deal of control over the placement and size of the object. You can move, resize, and format them as you want without affecting your worksheet data.

Basic Survival

Selecting an Object

To select an object, click once on it. When the object is selected, black selection handles appear along the borders of the object. Once the object is selected, you can move, resize, delete, or format it.

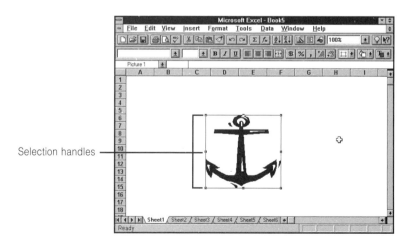

Selection handles

To select multiple objects, click on the first object. Then press and hold down the Shift key and click on the second object. Continue doing this until all the objects you want are selected.

Sometimes, you may accidentally select a cell in the worksheet instead of the object. To select the object, be sure to put the pointer right on the edge of the drawing. When the pointer is in the right spot, you see a small arrow. Alternatively, you can click on the Drawing Selection button ⬚ and then click on the object. Using this button, Excel selects only objects—not worksheet cells.

Moving an Object

If you want to move the object to another spot on the worksheet, you simply drag it to where you want it. Follow these steps:

1. Click once on the object to select it.

2. Point to any border of the object and drag the object to a new location. Be sure to point to a border, not a selection handle. Dragging the selection handle resizes the object, as described next. The pointer is in the right spot for moving when it looks like a small arrow.

To copy: hold down CTrl and drag

To move the object to another sheet or workbook, select the object and then select the Edit Cut command. Move to the new sheet or workbook and select the Edit Paste command.

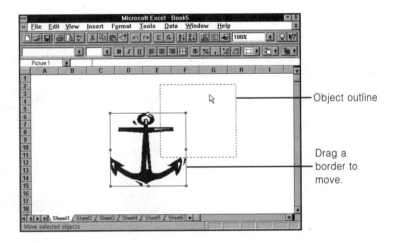

Object outline

Drag a border to move.

Resizing an Object

If you want to change the size of the object, follow these steps:

1. Click once on the object to select it.

2. Point to one of the black selection handles. When the pointer is in the right spot, it changes to a two-headed arrow.

3. Drag the handle to resize the object. As you drag you see an outline of the object.

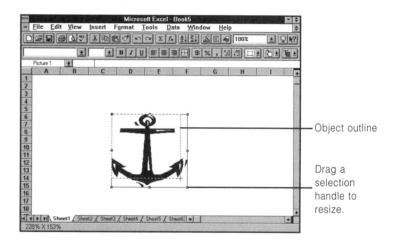

Object outline

Drag a selection handle to resize.

4. Release the mouse button when the object is the size you want.

Deleting an Object

If you have an object that you no longer want to include, or if you are working with the drawing tools and make a mistake, you can delete the object. To do so, simply follow these steps:

1. Click once on the object to select it.

2. Press the Delete key. Excel deletes the object.

Beyond Survival

Formatting an Object

You can tinker with the look of an object by changing its formatting. You can, for instance, change the pattern and color of the background of the object. If you don't like the line style used, you can select a different line style or thickness. To format an object, follow these steps:

1. Double-click on the object, or click once on the object and select the Format Object command. The Format Object dialog box appears.

2. Click on the Patterns tab.

Select a border here. 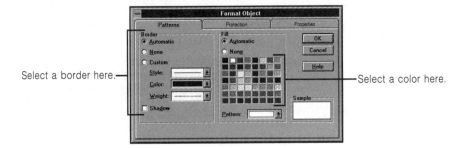 Select a color here.

3. To use a different border, click on the Custom button and then select a style from the Style drop-down list, a Color from the color palette, and a weight from the Weight drop-down list. If you want a drop shadow, check the Shadow check box.

4. To use a different pattern, click on a color for the background from the color palette. Then display the Pattern palette and click on a pattern.

5. Click OK, and Excel formats the object.

Background pattern added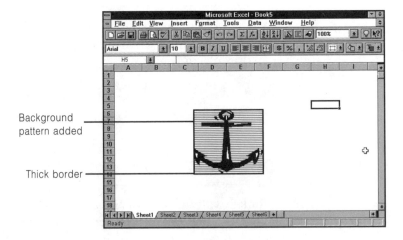

Thick border

Arranging Objects

When you draw one object and then add a second, the second one is placed on top. If you want, you can change the order of the two objects. To move the top object to the back, click the Send To Back button ![Send To Back icon]. To move the bottom object to the front, click the Bring To Front button ![Bring To Front icon].

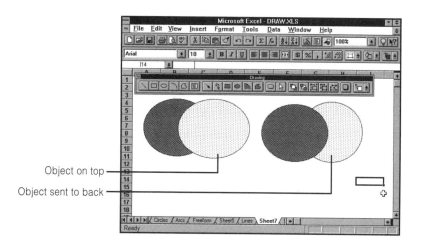

Object on top

Object sent to back

Grouping an Object

Using the buttons on the Drawing toolbar, you can combine simple shapes to create a drawing. When the drawing is complete, you may want to group each of the shapes into one object. Doing so will make it easy to select the entire drawing and then move, resize, or delete it. To group a set of objects, follow these steps:

1. Click on the first object you want to group.

2. Hold down the Shift key and click on the next object you want to select. Do this for each object you want to select. (If you click on the Drawing Selection button ![Drawing Selection icon] first and then click on the objects, it's easier to select objects—you can't accidentally select cells.)

3. Click on the Group button ![Group icon]. Word groups all the selected objects into one object. Notice that the selection handles enclose the entire set of objects.

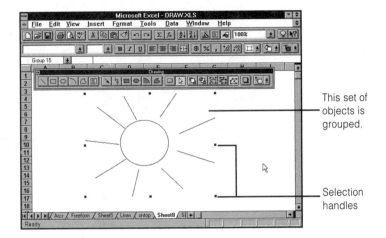

This set of
objects is
grouped.

Selection
handles

To ungroup the objects, select the group and click on the Ungroup
button .

Cheat Sheet

Creating a Chart

1. Select the range you want to chart.
2. Click the ChartWizard button .
3. Drag across a blank area of the worksheet.
4. Release the mouse button.
5. Make selections in the dialog boxes and keep clicking on Next until you come to the Step 5 of 5 dialog box.
6. In the Step 5 of 5 dialog box, change any options and click Finish.

Changing the Chart Type

1. Click once on the chart.
2. Click on the drop-down arrow next to the Chart Type button.
3. Click the new chart type you want.

Changing Charted Data

1. Double-click on the chart.
2. Click on the data point you want to change.
3. Drag the point up or down.

45

Creating Charts

Looking at column after column and row after row of numbers can be tiresome. To summarize the data or to show trends, you may want to use a visual representation of the data—that is, chart the data. Excel makes it easy to chart data by including a ChartWizard. This feature leads you step by step through the process of creating a chart.

Basic Survival

Understanding Chart Types

When you create a chart, Excel selects a column chart by default. However, you aren't limited to just this chart type. Excel provides 14 chart types to choose from, and each chart has several subtypes, or styles. Before you create a chart, you may want to take a look at the different chart types so you know what kind you want. The following list summarizes the different chart types.

- **Area chart** Use this chart when you want to show change in volume or magnitude over time.

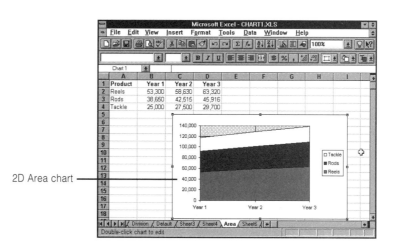

2D Area chart

- **3D Area chart**   Shows a 3D view of an area chart.

- **Bar chart**   This chart is useful when you want to compare items. The values are plotted horizontally (as opposed to a column chart where the values are plotted vertically). The horizontal plotting puts more emphasis on comparison, rather than time. Subtypes of this chart type include a stacked bar chart (values are stacked on each other) and 100% stacked (the percentage of each value is stacked).

- **3D Bar chart**   Shows a 3D view of a bar chart.

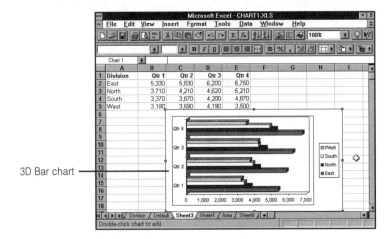

3D Bar chart ——

- **Column chart** (default chart type)   Use this chart when you want to compare items to emphasize change over time. The values are charted vertically. Subtypes include a stacked and 100% stacked chart, similar to their bar type counterparts.

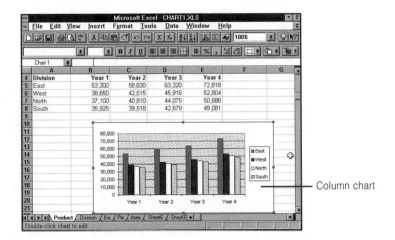

—— Column chart

- **3D Column chart** Shows a 3D view of a column chart.

- **Line chart** Use this chart type when you want to show trends or emphasize change over time. This chart type is similar to an area chart, but whereas an area chart emphasizes the amount of change, the line chart emphasizes the rate of change. Subtypes of the line chart include high-low-close-open (useful for charting stock prices).

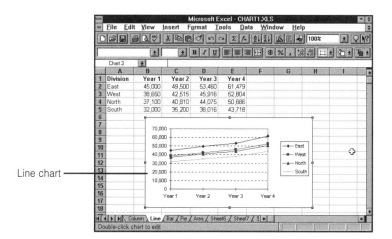

Line chart

- **3D Line chart** Shows a 3D view of a line chart. Ribbons are used for the lines.

- **Pie chart** Use this chart when you want to show the relationship of the values to the whole. You can chart only one data series in a pie chart.

- **3D Pie chart** Shows a 3D view of a pie chart.

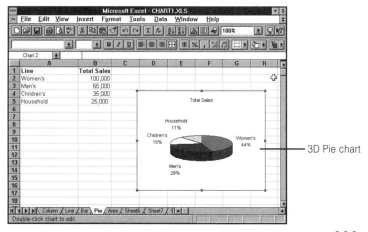

3D Pie chart

- **Doughnut chart**   Use this chart when you want to show more than one data series and show the relationship of the values to the whole.

- **Radar chart**   Use this chart when you want to show changes relative to a center point.

- **XY Scatter chart**   This chart type is useful for charting scientific data. It shows the relationship of values in several chart data series.

- **3D Surface chart**   Similar to a topographical map, this chart type is useful for finding relationships that may be otherwise difficult to see.

Creating a Chart

If you are worried about the difficulties in creating a chart, don't be. Excel provides a ChartWizard that leads you step by step through the process.

You can place a chart directly on the worksheet or, if you'd prefer, on a separate sheet. Depending on where you are placing the chart, you follow a slightly different starting procedure. But in both cases, you use the Chart Wizard.

Follow these steps:

1. Select the range that you want to chart. If your worksheet contains Total columns or rows, don't include them; they will throw the chart out of balance. For instance, if you are charting the sales of three divisions over four quarters, you want to chart and compare the individual values for each division and each quarter, not the total.

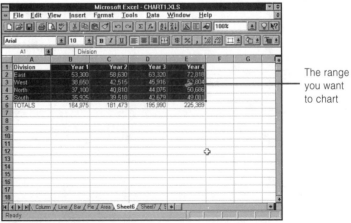

The range you want to chart

2. If you want to insert the chart on this worksheet, click on the ChartWizard button [icon].

If you want to insert the chart on a new sheet, select the Insert Chart command. Then select As New Sheet and skip to step 4.

3. Drag across a blank area of the worksheet to tell Excel where to place the embedded chart.

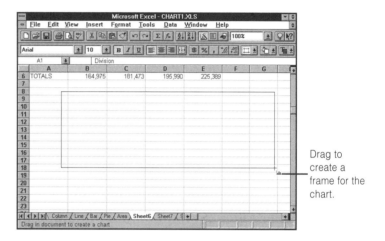

Drag to create a frame for the chart.

4. When you release the mouse button, you see the ChartWizard - Step 1 of 5 dialog box. Here you are prompted to confirm the selected range. Click on the Next button if the range is correct, or select a different range and click on Next. You see the ChartWizard - Step 2 of 5 dialog box.

Click Back To go backwards Through ChartWizard

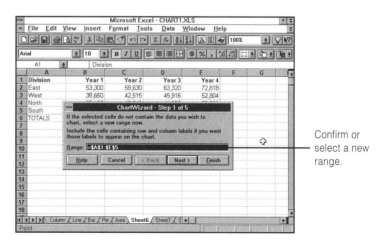

Confirm or select a new range.

5. Click on a chart type and then click on Next. The ChartWizard -
Step 3 of 5 dialog box appears.

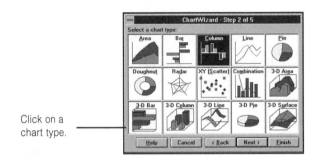

Click on a
chart type.

6. Click on a chart format and then click on Next. You see the
ChartWizard - Step 4 of 5 dialog box.

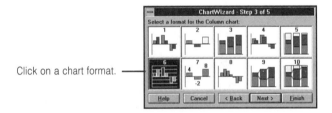

Click on a chart format.

7. Change any of the following and then click on Next:

- Select how the data series are charted: in Rows or in Columns.

- Select which row/column to use as the x-axis labels.

- Select which row/column to use for the legend.

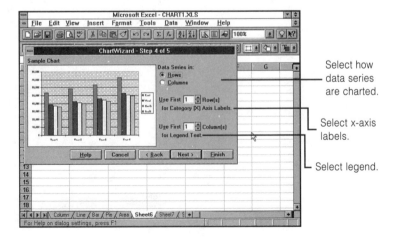

Select how
data series
are charted.

Select x-axis
labels.

Select legend.

8. In the ChartWizard - Step 5 of 5 dialog box, change any of the following and then click on Finish:

- Select whether you want to include a legend.

- If you want a chart title, type the title in the Chart Title text box.

- If you want axis titles, type them in the Category and Value text boxes.

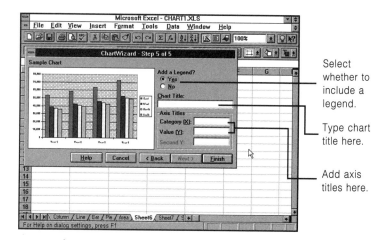

Select whether to include a legend.

Type chart title here.

Add axis titles here.

Excel creates the chart.

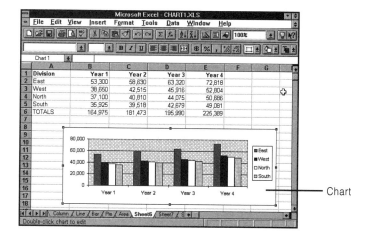

Chart

Selecting and Editing the Chart

Click once To edit an objecT Double-click To edit a charT

When you want to edit the chart object (move it, resize it, or delete it), click once on the chart object. Black selection handles appear around the edges of the chart frame. For information on editing the chart object, see the preceding chapter.

When you want to change elements of the chart (change the chart pattern, add a chart title, and so on), double-click on the chart. A grayish border appears around the edges of the chart. The next chapter explains how to format the chart elements.

Using the Chart Toolbar

When you are working on a chart, the Chart toolbar is displayed. The following table explains each of the buttons on this toolbar.

Button	Description
	Use this button to display a drop-down list of chart types. The 14 chart types are included in the palette. If you want to use a subtype, you need to use the command method to change the chart type (see the next section).
	Use this button to return the chart to the default chart type (column chart).
	Use this button to start the ChartWizard.
	Click this button to hide/display horizontal gridlines.
	Click this button to hide/display the legend.

Beyond Survival

Changing the Chart Type

Charting is one of those skills you learn by doing. At first, you probably won't be sure of what you want to show or what your message is. However, after you create the chart and see the data represented visually, you'll have a better idea of the message and the best way to convey that message. You can then change the chart type by following these steps:

1. Click once on the chart to select it.

2. Click on the drop-down arrow next to the Chart Type button. You see a drop-down list of chart types.

Click on the chart type you want.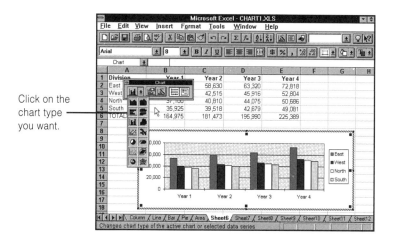

3. Click on the new chart type you want.

If you want to use one of the subchart types, you need to use the command method to change the chart type. Follow these steps:

1. Double-click on the chart.

2. Select the Format Chart Type command. You see the Chart Type dialog box.

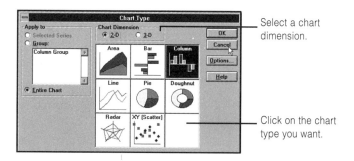

Select a chart dimension.

Click on the chart type you want.

3. Select a chart dimension: 2D or 3D. Excel displays the available chart choices.

4. Click on the chart type you want.

5. Click OK.

Changing Charted Data

The chart is linked to the worksheet data, so when you make a change in the worksheet, the chart is updated. If you want to change a value in the worksheet, edit it as you do normally. The chart will instantly be updated to reflect the change.

If you delete data in the worksheet, the matching data series will be deleted in the chart. If you want, you can delete the series from the chart, but leave the data in the worksheet. Click on the data series that you want to delete and press the Delete key.

Changing the Worksheet Data by Changing the Chart

Keep in mind that the worksheet and chart are connected. Just as you can change the worksheet data to update the chart, you can also change the chart to update the worksheet data. To make this type of change, follow these steps:

1. Double-click on the chart.

2. Click on the data point you want to change. When a single data point is selected, black selection handles appear along the borders of the area.

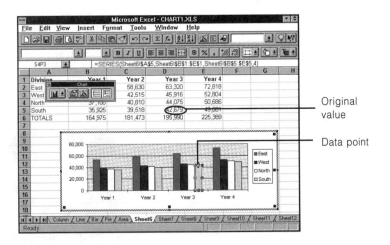

Original value

Data point

3. Drag the data point up or down. The resulting worksheet data is updated to reflect the change.

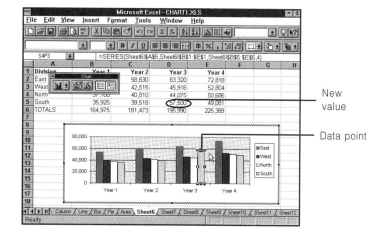

New value

Data point

Cheat Sheet

Changing the Series Pattern

1. Double-click on the chart.
2. Click the chart series you want to change.
3. Select Format Selected Series.
4. Click the Patterns tab.
5. Click the color you want to use.
6. Click the down-arrow next to the Pattern list and then click the pattern you want.
7. Click OK.

Adding Chart Titles

1. Double-click the chart to activate it.
2. Select Insert Titles.
3. Check the kind of title you want displayed.

Formatting the Legend

1. Double-click the chart.
2. Double-click the legend.
3. Click the Font tab.
4. Select the options you want.
5. Click OK.

46

Formatting Charts

Many different elements make up a chart—the data points, the collection of data points or series, the axes, the legend, and more. You have great control over each of these chart elements. You can change each individual element of the chart.

Excel offers many chart formatting features. This chapter covers the features for the changes you will most often make. For complete information on all features, see your Excel manual.

Basic Survival

Changing the Series Pattern

ShorTcuT:
Double-click
on The series
To change

Each set of data points is grouped into a series and is represented in the chart using a predefined pattern. For instance, all of the East division sales appear in one color and pattern. If you don't like the pattern used, you can change it by following these steps:

1. Double-click on the chart.

2. Click the chart series that you want to change. Selection handles appear around each of the data points in the series.

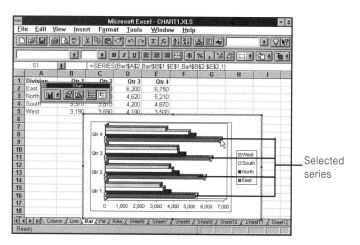

Selected series

3. Select the Format Selected Data Series command.

4. Click on the Patterns tab. You see the Patterns tab of the Format Data Series dialog box.

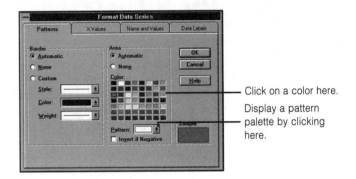

Click on a color here.

Display a pattern palette by clicking here.

5. Click on the color you want to use.

6. Click on the down arrow next to the Pattern list and then click on the pattern you want to use.

7. Click OK. Excel uses the selected pattern and color.

Adding Chart Titles

Your reader may not understand what the chart represents without explanatory text—for instance, a chart title and axes titles. You can add a title that explains the purpose of your chart and add text along the axes. You can format these titles any way you choose.

Follow these steps to add chart titles:

1. Double-click on the chart to activate it.

2. Select the Insert Titles command. You see the Titles dialog box.

Check the type of title you want to add.

3. Check the kind of title you want displayed: Chart Title, Value Z Axis, Category X Axis, or Series Y Axis. Depending on the chart type, you may not have options for all three axes.

4. Click OK. Excel adds a title and displays filler text.

5. Type the text and press Enter. Excel adds the title.

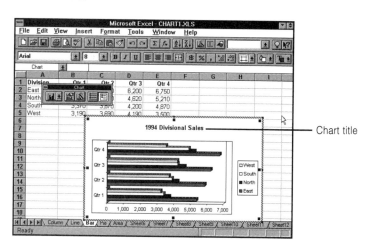

Chart title

Formatting the Legend

When you create a chart, a legend is added by default (it's placed on the right side of the chart). If you don't like the default colors, placement, font, and border, you can change them. To make any changes, follow these steps:

1. Double-click the chart to activate it.

2. Double-click on the legend. You see the Format Legend dialog box.

3. Click on the Font tab and do any of the following:

- Select a font from the Font list.

- Select a style from the Font Style list.

- Select a size from the Size list.

- Select a color from the Color list.

Select the font you want.

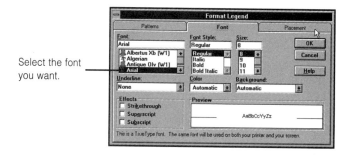

315

4. If you want to change the border or pattern, click on the Patterns tab and do one of the following:

- To use a different border, click on the Custom button and then select a style from the Style drop-down list, a color from the color palette, and a weight from the Weight drop-down list. If you want to use a drop shadow, check the Shadow check box.

- To use a different pattern, click on a color for the background from the color palette. Then display the Pattern palette and click on a pattern.

5. If you want to change the position of the legend, click on the Placement tab. Then click on the placement you want: Bottom, Corner, Top, Right, or Left.

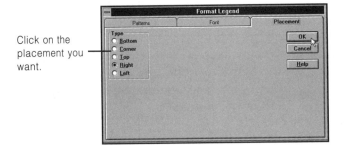

Click on the placement you want.

6. Click OK. Excel formats the legend.

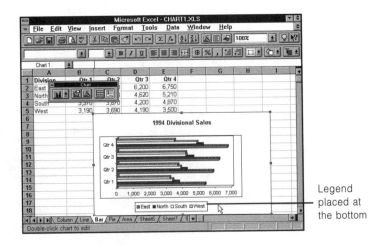

Legend placed at the bottom

Beyond Survival

Changing the Series Order

Excel will chart the series in the order they appear in the worksheet. In some cases, you may prefer a different order. For example, in the following figure the first series is the largest, which causes it to over-shadow the series behind it. You can adjust the series so that they are in ascending order.

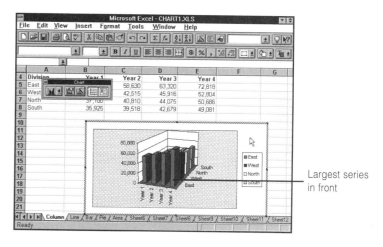

Largest series in front

To change the series order, follow these steps:

1. Double-click on the chart to edit it.

2. Select the Format **1** *Column* Group command. The word in italic will vary depending on the chart type.

3. Click on the Series Order tab.

4. Click on the series you want to move; then click the Move Up or Move Down buttons.

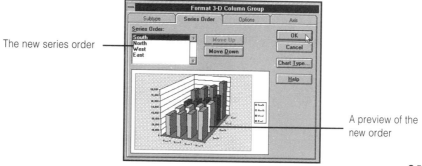

The new series order

A preview of the new order

317

5. Click OK. Excel adjusts the series.

Overlapping Series and Changing the Gap Width

Excel puts each series next to each other and spaces the series out evenly across the chart. You may want to overlap the series or change the amount of space between each set of data series. To do so, follow these steps:

1. Double-click on the chart to edit it.

2. Select the Format **1** *Column* Group command. The word in italic will vary depending on the chart type.

3. Click on the Options tab.

4. If you want to overlap the series, type a value in the Overlap text box or use the spin arrows to select a value.

5. If you want to change the width between the data series, type a value in the Gap Width text box or use the spin arrows to select a value.

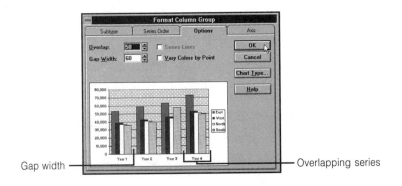

Gap width ———   ——— Overlapping series

6. Click OK. Excel formats the series accordingly.

Adding Series Labels

You may want to add text to each series to show its value or overall percentage. These labels can make the chart more informative. To add series labels, follow these steps:

1. Double-click on the chart.

2. Click on the chart series that you want to change.

3. Select the Format Selected Data Series command.

4. Click on the Data Labels tab.

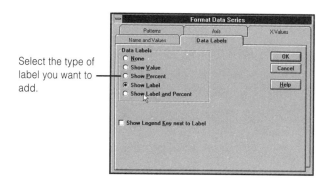

Select the type of label you want to add.

5. Select what you want to show: value, percent, label, or label and percent. Depending on the chart type, some of the options may not be available.

6. If you want to show a small legend key next to the values, check the Show Legend Key next to the Label check box.

7. Click OK. Excel adds the labels.

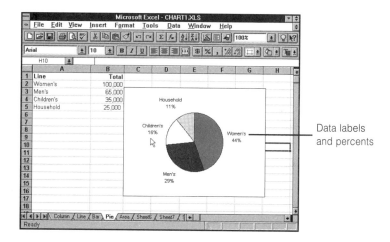

Data labels and percents

Changing the Plot Area

The plot area in a 2D chart is the area bounded by the axes (basically, the background grid). The plot area for a 3D chart includes the category names, tick-mark labels, and axis titles. 3D charts also have walls and a floor. The chart area is the entire chart, including legends. You can change the colors and patterns used for each of these areas. To do so, follow these steps:

1. Double-click on the chart to activate it.

2. Click on the area you want to change.

ShorTcuT:
Double-click on
The charT area
To change

3. Select the Format command. Then select one of the following commands:

- Selected Plot Area

- Selected Walls

- Selected Chart Area

You see the Format Plot Area dialog box. The name of the command and dialog box will vary, depending on the area you selected in step 2.

Select a border here.

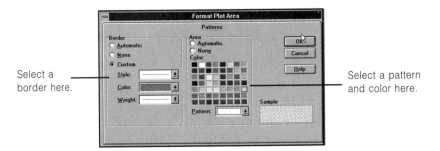

Select a pattern and color here.

4. If you want to use a different border, click on the Custom button and then select a style from the Style drop-down list, a color from the color palette, and a weight from the Weight drop-down list. If you want to use a drop shadow, check the Shadow check box.

5. If you want to use a different pattern, click on a color for the background from the color palette. Then display the Pattern palette and click on a pattern.

6. Click OK. Excel makes the change.

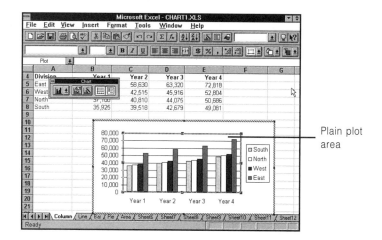

Plain plot area

Formatting the Axes

The axes make up the grid on which the data is plotted. On a 2D chart, the y-axis is the vertical axis, and the x-axis is the horizontal axis. A 3D chart has three axes: the y-axis is the front to back axis, the x-axis is the left to right axis, and the z axis is the bottom to top axis.

You can control all the aspects of the axes: the appearance of the line, the tick marks, the number format used, and more. To make changes, follow these steps:

1. Double-click the chart to activate it.

2. Double-click on the axis that you want to format. You see the Format Axis dialog box.

3. To change the pattern, click on the Patterns tab. Then do any of the following:

• To use a different border, click on the Custom button and then select a style from the Style drop-down list, a color from the color palette, and a weight from the Weight drop-down list.

• Select the placement of the major and minor tick marks (None, Inside, Outside, or Cross).

• Select where to place the tick-mark labels: None, High, Low, or Next to Axis.

321

Select a line
style here.

Select tick mark
placement here.

4. To change the number format, click on the Number tab. Select the numeric format that you want to use.

Click on the
number format
you want.

5. To change the scale, click on the Scale tab. Then enter the minimum value, maximum value, major unit, and minor unit. For example, if you think the values on your axis are too close together, you may want to enter a larger major unit (for instance, show only every 20,000 rather than every 10,000).

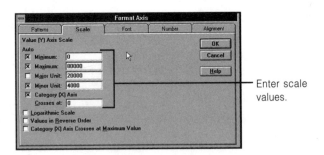

Enter scale
values.

6. Click OK, and Excel formats the axes.

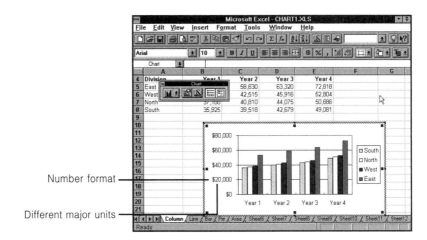

Number format

Different major units

Cheat Sheet

Understanding a Database

- A database stores a set of related information.
- A record contains all the information about one subject.
- Records are entered in rows.
- Each type of information is stored in a field.
- Fields are stored in columns.

Creating a Database

- Enter the field headings in the top row.
- Make a preliminary sketch.
- Use unique names.

Entering Data

1. Select Data Form.
2. Click OK if necessary.
3. Type an entry for the first field and press Tab.
4. Type an entry for the next field and press Tab.
5. Click the New button.
6. Continue typing information and clicking New until all records are added.
7. Click Close.

Editing Data

1. Select Data Form.
2. Scroll to the record you want to change.
3. Make any changes.
4. Click Close.

47

Creating Databases

In addition to keeping track of numbers, you can use Excel as a simple data management program. You can keep track of clients, products, and inventories in an Excel worksheet. Excel provides many data management tools for working with lists of data.

Basic Survival

Understanding a Database

A *database* is a set of related information about a particular person, transaction, or event. For instance, you could keep a database listing your products. The list could include the company name, product name, product type, and price. Or, you could keep a list of clients with the client's name, address, and phone number.

Record = row

One set of information is called a *record*. For instance, the record for client Frances McCarthy would include his name, address, and phone number. In Excel, records are entered in rows.

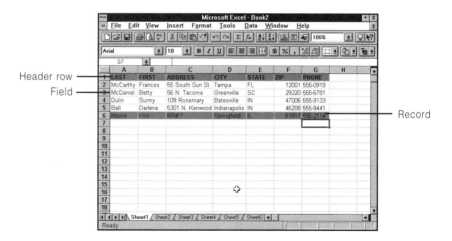

Header row —
Field —
Record

Field = column

Each individual piece of information in a database is stored in a *field*. For instance, the LAST field might contain the last name of each client. In Excel, the fields are stored in columns.

Creating a Database

To create a database, you simply enter the field headings in the top row. These headings indicate the names of the fields you want to include. As you enter the header row, keep these points in mind:

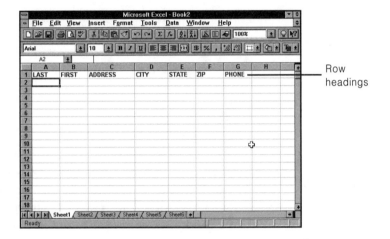

Row headings

- Take some time to sketch out the information that you want to include in your database. If you want to sort on a particular field, be sure to include a separate column for that field. For instance, if you want to sort by last name, include separate fields for first and last name.

- Be sure to use unique names for each column. Excel can get confused if you use the same name in more than one column.

- It's best to store the database in its own worksheet. You can have a database on a worksheet with other types of information, but because you'll want to sort and possibly rearrange the database, it's usually best to keep the database separate.

- The database is an ordinary worksheet. You use the same procedure to format the column headings, insert columns, and move and copy data.

- It's a good idea to make the column headings stand out—for instance, make them bold—so that you don't confuse the headings with the actual data within the database.

Entering Data

If you like the regular worksheet style of entering data, you can just enter data directly in the rows. Select the cell and then type the entry. After you complete the entries for the first record (all the columns for that record), move to the next row to add the next record. You can insert rows to add new records.

If you prefer, you can display a data form on-screen and enter the records in that form. To do so, follow these steps:

1. Select the Data Form command.

2. Click OK if asked whether the first row is the header row. You see the data form on-screen.

Type the information here.

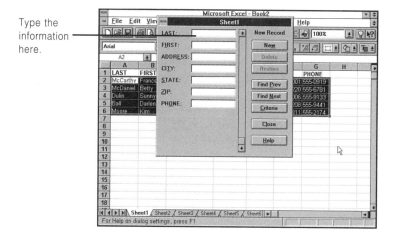

3. Type the entry for the first field and press Tab. You can type more information than the field in the data form will show. As you type, the information scrolls to the left.

4. Type the entry for the next field and press Tab. You can also press Shift+Tab to move backwards through the fields. Do this for each field in the record.

5. To add the new record and display a blank form, click on the New button. Excel adds a row to the worksheet; the data form is still displayed on-screen.

6. Continue typing information in each field and clicking New until you add all the records you want.

7. Click Close. You are returned to the worksheet.

Editing Data

You can edit a field directly in the record row and field column, or you can use the data form to edit a record. To edit a field, select the cell you want to change. Remember that records are stored in rows; fields in columns. Double-click the cell, make any changes, and press Enter. If you make a mistake and don't want to make the entry, press Esc rather than Enter.

To use the data form to edit a record, follow these steps:

1. Select the Data Form command.

2. Click on the scroll arrows to display the record you want to change. Or, click on the Find Prev or Find Next buttons until the record you want is displayed.

Excel keeps track of the number of records you enter in a database. The current record number and total record number are displayed in the upper right corner of the data form—for instance, 2 of 3. This information may help you find the record you want.

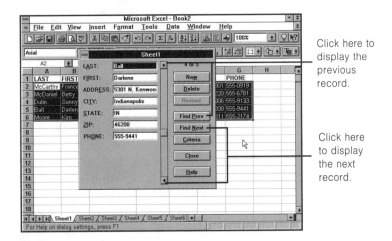

Click here to display the previous record.

Click here to display the next record.

3. Make any changes.

4. Click Close.

Deleting Records

To delete a record in the worksheet, click on the row number to select the entire row, and then select the Edit Delete command. The row and the information are deleted from the worksheet.

*Cannot undo
The record
deleTion!*

To delete a record using the data form, follow these steps:

1. Select the Data Form command.

2. Display the record you want to delete.

3. Click on the Delete button. Excel prompts you to confirm the deletion.

4. Click OK, and Excel deletes the record.

Cheat Sheet

Finding Data

1. Select Data Form.
2. Click the Criteria button.
3. Move to the field you want to search.
4. Enter a text entry to find a specific match.
5. Click Find Next.

Sorting Data

1. Select Data Sort.
2. Display the Sort By drop-down list and click the column you want to search first.
3. Click Ascending or Descending order.
4. Click OK.

Filtering Data

1. Select Data Filter AutoFilter.
2. Move to the column heading for the column you want to filter.
3. Display the drop-down list to see the entries.
4. Select the records you want to match.
5. Click OK.

48

Working with Databases

Once you have set up a database, Excel provides many tools for working with the data. For instance, you can quickly search the database to find the record you want. You can also sort the records to display them in an order you want. To display only a certain set of records, you can filter the database. And finally, you can subtotal sorted data. This chapter discusses all of these database features.

Basic Survival

Finding Data

Instead of wasting time trying to look through each record to find the one you want, search for the record. Follow these steps:

1. Select the Data Form command.

2. Click on the Criteria button. You will see a blank record on-screen.

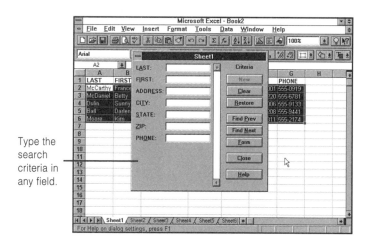

Type the
search
criteria in
any field.

3. Move to the field on which you want to search. For instance, if you know the last name of a client, move to the last name field. Or, if you want to list all clients in Indiana, move to the State field.

4. Enter a text entry to find a specific match. You can type all or part of the entry. For instance, if you want to find the client Samson, you could type Samson, Sams, or Sa.

You can also type a comparison formula. For instance, to find all values over 250 in an inventory database, you'd move to the units field and type >250. Here are the comparison operators you can use:

Operator	Meaning	Example
>	Greater than	>250 (Finds all values greater than 250.)
<	Less than	<250 (Finds all values less than 250.)
=	Equal to	=250 (Finds all values that are exactly 250.)
<=	Less than or equal to	<=250 (Finds all values that are 250 or less.)
>=	Greater than or equal to	>=250 (Finds all values that are 250 or more.)
<>	Not	<>250 (Finds all values that are not 250.)

Find all states that match IN.

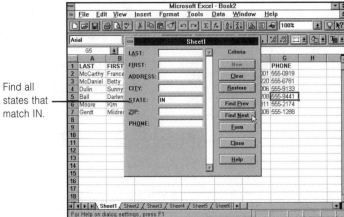

5. Click on the Find Next button. Excel displays the first matching record. Continue clicking on the Find Next button until the record you want is displayed.

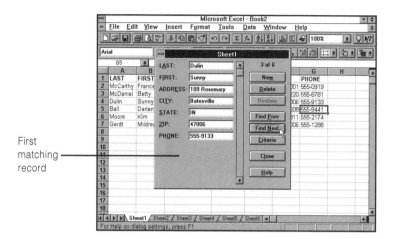

First
matching —
record

If Excel doesn't find a match, you'll hear a beep, and Excel will return to the data form. There are a number of reasons why Excel might not be able to find a match for the data you selected. Check your spelling, in case you misspelled the word, and try the search again. Also, rather than typing the entire value, try typing a partial value or using a comparison formula.

Sorting Data

Sort Ascending button and Sort Descending button sort by the first column.

It's easy to change the order of your database. Do you like the names arranged alphabetically? Then sort on the last name field. Do you want to sort by ZIP code? Then sort on the ZIP code field. You can even search on more than one column at once: for instance, sort first by name, and then by ZIP code.

To sort the database, select any cell within the database and then follow these steps:

1. Select the Data Sort command. You see the Sort dialog box.

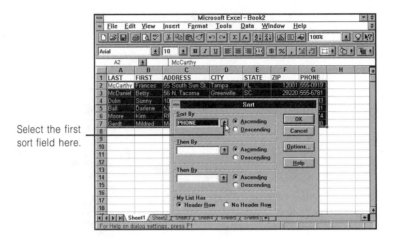

Select the first
sort field here.

2. Display the Sort By drop-down list and click on the field that you
want to sort by first. For instance, if you were sorting by last
names, you'd select last name from this list.

If the Header Row option button is selected, Excel uses the
column headings as choices in the drop-down list, and Excel will
not include this header row in the sort. If you don't have column
headings, you can have Excel display the first value in the column
in the drop-down list. To do so, click the No Header Row option
button so that Excel will include the first row.

3. Click on Ascending or Descending order.

4. To sort on a second field, display the Then By drop-down list,
click on the column, and then click on a sort order. The following
sort options will sort first by last name and then by ZIP code.

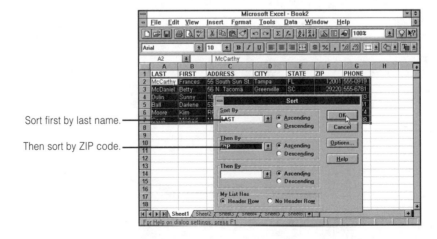

Sort first by last name.

Then sort by ZIP code.

5. To sort on a third field, display the Then By drop-down list, click on the column, and then click on a sort order.

6. Click OK. Excel sorts the database in the order you selected.

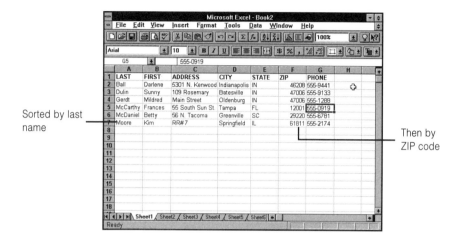

Sorted by last name

Then by ZIP code

Beyond Survival

Filtering Data

Filtering data is an easy way to work with a subset of data. Suppose you had a product database and wanted to show only products from one company. You could search for that company and display the records one by one. However, an easier way is to filter the database so that only those records are displayed.

To turn on AutoFilter, follow these steps:

1. Select the Data Filter AutoFilter command. Drop-down arrows appear next to each column in your database.

Filter arrows

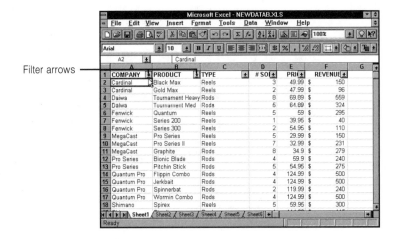

2. Move to the column heading for the column by which you want to filter. For example, if you wanted to filter a product database to display only a certain product type, you'd move to the TYPE column.

3. To display the drop-down list, click on the arrow or press Alt+↓. You will see a list of entries.

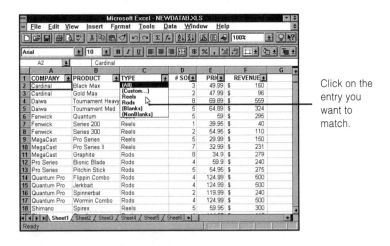

Click on the entry you want to match.

4. Select the records you want to match:

Option	Description
(All)	Displays all records in that column.
(Custom…)	Displays the Custom dialog box and enters a custom filter.
Value	Displays only records that match the specific value you select.
(Blanks)	Displays only rows that are blank in this column.
(NonBlanks)	Displays only rows that contain values in this column.

5. If necessary, click OK. Excel displays only those records that meet the selected criteria. All other rows are still in the database; they are just hidden. You can tell the database has been filtered because the filter arrow is a different color.

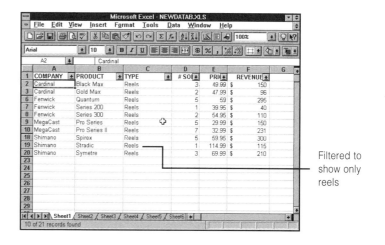

Filtered to show only reels

Important! To display all records again, select the Data Filter AutoFilter command so that there isn't a check mark next to it. The drop-down arrows disappear, and all records are displayed.

Adding Subtotals

Subtotals are an easy way to summarize data in a list. With previous versions of Excel, users had to manually insert a subtotal row and create the formula. With Excel 5, you just select the Data Subtotals command. Excel creates the formula, inserts the subtotal and grand total rows, and outlines the data automatically.

Before you can create the subtotals, you need to sort the database. For instance, if you wanted to subtotal each category in a checkbook database, you'd sort on the category. (See the section "Sorting Data" for information on sorting.) Once the records are in the proper order, Excel can create the subtotals.

Follow these steps:

1. Select the Data Subtotals command. You see the Subtotal dialog box.

Select how you want
to group the data.

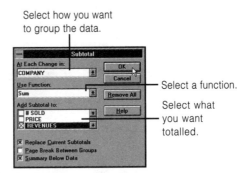

Select a function.

Select what
you want
totalled.

2. Select the columns you want subtotalled from the At Each Change in drop-down list. For instance, if you want each company subtotalled, you'd select the COMPANY column here.

3. Select the function you want performed. The most common is Sum, but you can select other functions.

4. In the Add Subtotal to list, check the boxes that you want subtotalled. For example, you don't want the COMPANY fields subtotalled here. You'd want the revenue amount, so check REVENUE. You can check more than one check box to have Excel calculate the function on each selected field.

5. If you want to replace any existing subtotals, uncheck the Replace Current Subtotals check box.

6. If you want to insert a page break before each group, check the Page Break Between Groups check box.

7. By default, the subtotal and grand totals appear at the end of the data group. If you prefer to show these totals before the data group, check the Summary Below Data.

8. Click OK. Excel inserts a subtotal row for each time the selected field changes, and performs the selected function on the column you asked to total. In the product example, Excel would create a subtotal for each company and then subtotal revenues for each company. A grand total is displayed at the end of the database.

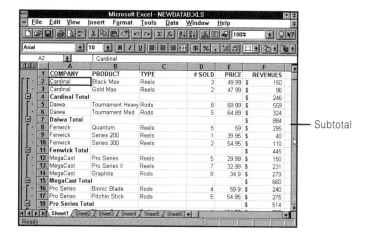

Subtotal

To remove the subtotals, select the Data Subtotals command, and then click on the Remove All button.

Cheat Sheet

Recording a Macro

1. Select Tools Record Macro Record New Macro.
2. Type a name in the Macro Name text box.
3. Click OK.
4. Perform the commands you want to record in the macro.
5. Click the Stop Recording button.

Running a Macro

1. Select Tools Macro.
2. Click the name of the macro you want.
3. Click the Run button.

Assigning the Macro to a Shortcut Key or Menu

1. Select Tools Macro.
2. Click the macro you want to change.
3. Click the Options button.
4. To add the macro to the Tools menu, click the Menu Item on Tools Menu check box.
5. To assign the macro to a shortcut key, check the Shortcut Key check box.
6. Click OK.
7. Click Close.

49

Creating Macros

If you perform the same task over and over again, you can record a macro to do the task for you with one key press. For example, suppose that you regularly select a database, sort the columns, and print the report. Each time you do this, you select the Data Sort command, enter a sort order, choose OK, and select File Print. You can record a macro that does all this for you in one step. All you need to do is create the macro and then run it when you need it.

If the actions you want to record are style changes (making an entry bold, changing the number format, using a different font, etc.), you can also create a style. A *style* is a collection of formats that you can apply to other cells in the worksheet. See Chapter 29, "Copying Formatting and Creating Styles."

Basic Survival

Recording a Macro

Even though using a macro sounds intimidating at first, you can easily record a macro using Excel. A *macro* is a set of VisualBasic programming commands. If you are a programmer, you can use this programming language to create powerful and complex programs. But you don't have to be a programmer or even know about programming commands to create a macro. You can use the Macro Recorder to create the macro and enter the commands automatically.

Follow these steps to create the macro:

1. Open the Tools menu and select the Record Macro command. Then select Record New Macro from the submenu to start the recorder. The Record New Macro dialog box appears.

Type the macro name here.

2. Type a name in the Macro Name text box.

3. Click OK. Excel displays the Stop Recording toolbar on-screen and displays **Recording** in the status bar.

Stop Recording toolbar ⟶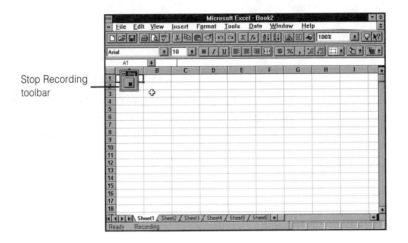

Remember:
Excel is
recording ALL
actions!

4. Perform the actions you want to record. Keep in mind that Excel is recording all your actions—any commands you select, text you type, or ranges you select will be included in the macro. Be sure to do only the steps you want recorded.

5. When you are finished recording the actions, click the Stop Recording button or select the Tools Record Macro Stop Recording command. Excel stops recording.

Note that when you create a macro, Excel creates a separate macro sheet, called Module 1, and stores the commands on that sheet. The macro sheet is saved when you save the workbook.

Running a Macro

It's a good idea to test the macro on a blank or sample worksheet before you run it on a real worksheet. If something goes wrong, you can spot the problem before you mess up real data. It's also a good idea to save the worksheet before you run the macro. If something goes wrong, you can abandon the worksheet and open the original saved version from the disk.

All your hard work spent creating a macro will pay off when you see how easy it is to replay the macro. Follow these steps to run a macro:

1. Select the Tools Macro command. You see the Macro dialog box.

2. Click on the name of the macro you want to run.

Click on the macro you want to run.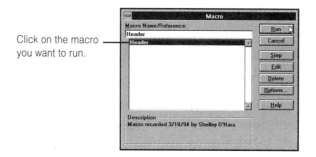

3. Click on the Run button. Excel performs the actions you recorded in the macro.

Beyond Survival

Deleting a Macro

If you no longer need a macro, you can delete it. Select the Tools Macro command, click on the macro you want to delete, and then click the Delete button.

Assigning the Macro to a Shortcut Key or Menu

If you want to be able to run the macro by pressing a shortcut key or by selecting it from an Excel menu, you can do so. Follow these steps:

1. Select the Tools Macro command. You see the Macro dialog box.

2. Click on the macro you want to change.

3. Click on the Options button. The Macro Options dialog box appears.

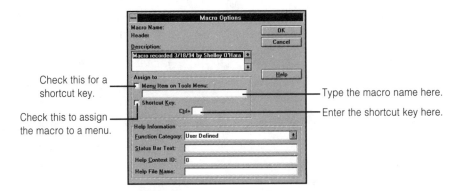

Check this for a shortcut key.

Check this to assign the macro to a menu.

Type the macro name here.

Enter the shortcut key here.

4. If you want to add this macro to the Tools menu, check the Menu Item on Tools Menu check box. Enter the name you want to appear on the menu. If you want a description to appear in the status bar when this command is selected, enter it in the Status Bar Text text box.

5. If you want to assign the macro to a shortcut key, check the Shortcut Key check box and type a letter in the Ctrl+ text box. (To run the macro, you will press Ctrl plus the letter you enter.)

6. Click OK.

7. Click Close. You can now run the macro by pressing the shortcut key (if you assigned one) or by opening the Tools menu and clicking on the macro command (if you added it to the menu).

Editing a Macro

Unless you are knowledgeable about VisualBasic programming language, the best way to edit a macro is probably to just re-record it. Select the Tools Record Macro Record New Macro command to start the recorder. Type the same name you used for the original macro in the Macro Name text box. Click OK. When you are prompted to replace the existing macro, click on the Yes button. Re-record the actions you want to save in the macro. Go slowly and try not to make the same mistake (if you know what the mistake was).

When you are finished recording, click the Stop Recording button. Test your macro on a blank or sample worksheet before you run it on a real worksheet.

If you want to edit or take a look at the macro commands, click on the Module 1 sheet tab to display the macro sheet. (You can also select the Tools Macro command, click on the macro you want to view, and click on the Edit button.)

Macro name — 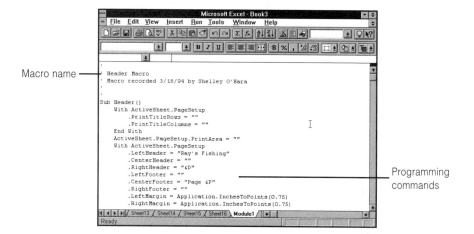 — Programming commands

You will see the programming commands that make up your macro. The macro consists of the keywords Sub and End Sub to indicate the start and end of the macro. Between these keywords you see the statements or commands.

Excel devotes an entire manual to the VisualBasic programming language. Review this manual for complete information on all the commands.

A

Installing Excel 5

These steps will guide you through the basic procedure for installing Microsoft Excel. Before installing, however, you should make copies of the disks. (To copy a disk, open File Manager from Program Manager's Main program group, and select Copy Disk from the Disk menu.) Then install Excel from the copies rather than from the originals, and keep the original disks in a safe place.

To install Excel 5 on your computer, follow these steps:

1. Start Microsoft Windows, if you haven't already.

2. Insert the first installation disk in the appropriate drive.

3. From Program Manager's File menu, select Run. The Run dialog box appears.

4. Type the drive letter, a colon, and **setup** in the Command Line text box. For example, if the disk is in drive A, you would type **a:setup**.

5. Click OK to begin the Excel Setup process.

6. Read the first dialog box that appears; then click OK to proceed.

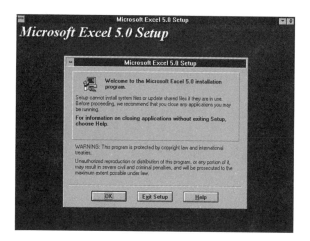

7. In the next dialog box, type your name and organization in the appropriate text boxes. Click OK to go to the next dialog box.

8. Click OK to confirm your name and organization.

9. The next dialog box shows your Product ID number. (You can see this number at any time after you install by selecting the About Microsoft Excel command from Excel's Help menu.) Click OK.

10. Next, specify the directory in which you want to store Excel's files. (The default is C:\EXCEL. If you want to designate a different directory, click on the Change Directory button, type a new directory, and then click OK.) Click OK to accept the specified directory.

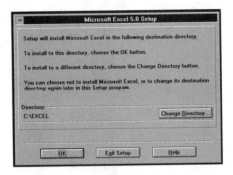

11. In the next dialog box, click the Typical button to install Excel's most common options.

12. Choose a program group in which to install the Excel files. (The default program group is Microsoft Office.) Click the Continue button to go on.

13. The Setup program checks for the necessary disk space and then begins the installation process. Dialog boxes appear when you need to insert new disks. Follow the on-screen instructions.

14. After all the Excel files have been copied to your computer, a dialog box appears, verifying that the setup was completed successfully. Click OK.

You will be returned to Program Manager, where the Microsoft Excel icon should be installed in the program group you selected in step 12. Turn to Chapter 1, "Starting Excel," for information on running the program.

B

Function Directory

Excel provides many functions that you can use to perform complex calculations. Functions are covered in detail in Chapter 13, "Entering Functions." This reference lists the commonly used functions as well as the form you use to enter them, called the *syntax*. Remember that a function consists of these parts:

An equal sign   Indicates a formula.

The function name   Is usually a shortened version of the function it performs.

Parentheses   Contain arguments.

Arguments   Are the values or cells you want used in the function. Some functions require no arguments; for some, you can enter more than one argument; and for some, arguments are optional.

For complete information on all available functions, see your Excel manual.

AVERAGE

=AVERAGE(number 1,number 2...)

Averages the numbers in parentheses. The numbers can be specific values, cells, or a range.

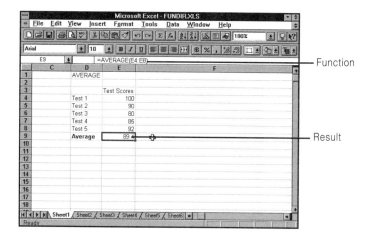

Function

Result

COUNT

=COUNT(value 1,value 2...)

Counts the values in parentheses. The values can be specific values, specific cells, or a range. Excel will only count values (numbers, dates, and times). It will not count text entries.

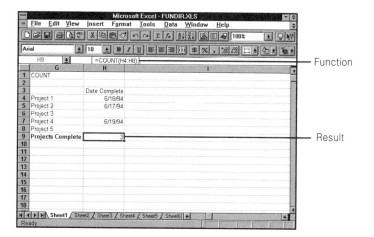

Function

Result

FV

=FV(rate,nper,pmt,pv,type)

Calculates the future value of an investment. For example, if you save $500 a month for 7 years at an interest rate of 6%, how much will you have saved?

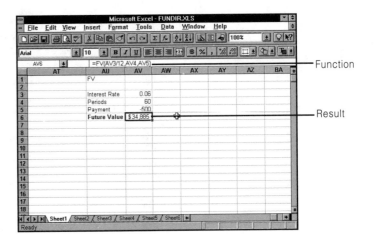

IF

=IF(logical_text,value_if_true,value_if_false)

Performs a logical test on two values and then displays one value if the test is true, another if the test is false. For instance, you could create a formula that checks the number of days a bill is past due. If the number is greater than 60, you could print a message asking for payment. If the number is 0 (payment has been made), you could include a message saying thanks for making the payment.

If you want to display a message, enter the text within quotation marks. If you want to use a formula to test for the true and false results, just type the formula.

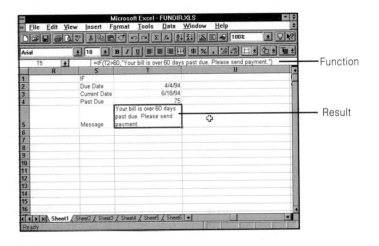

IPMT

=IPMT(rate,per,nper,pv,fv,type)

Calculates the interest paid during a single period of a loan.

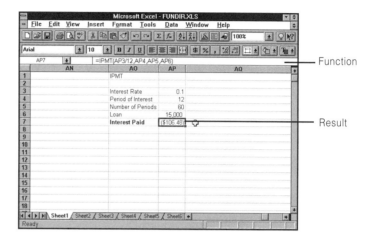

MAX

=MAX(value 1,value 2...)

Returns the largest value in a range.

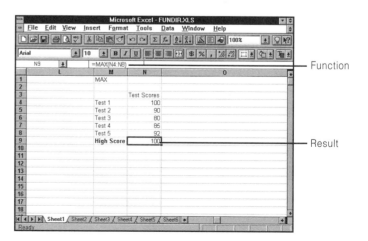

MIN

=MIN(value 1,value 2...)

Returns the lowest value in a range.

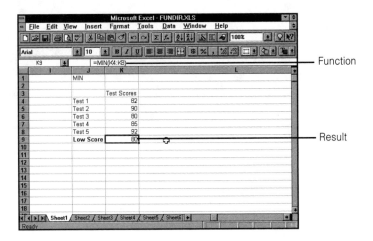

NA

=NA( )

Enters #NA in a cell so that it is clear which cells should contain values, but do not at this point.

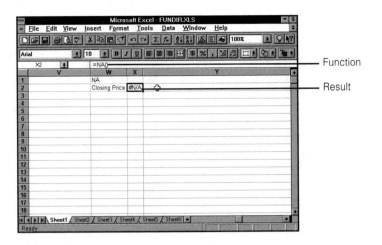

NOW

=NOW()

Enters the current date and time in the worksheet cell. Note that this function requires no arguments; you just enter the two parentheses.

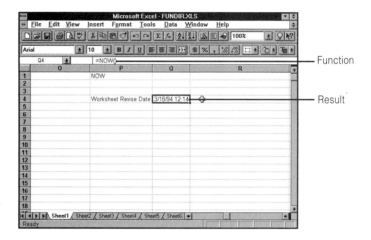

NPER

=NPER(rate,pmt,pv,fv,type)

Tells you how many payments you need to make on a loan.

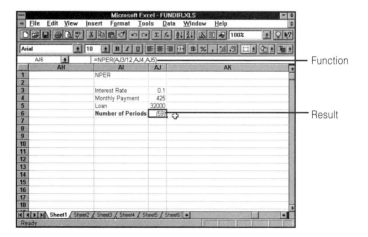

PMT

=PMT(rate,nper,pv,fv,type)

Figures the payment on a loan. Here are the arguments:

Argument	Description
rate	Interest rate. You have to match the rate to the term (nper). So if you are calculating a monthly payment and you have an annual interest rate of 10, you'd enter .1/12.
nper	Number of periods. A five year car loan has 60 monthly payments.
pv	Present value. The amount of the loan or the amount of money you want to invest.
fv	Future value. This argument is optional; when you leave it out, Excel assumes 0, which is usually what you want.
type	When payments are made. This argument is optional. Use 1 for payments you make at the beginning of the period. Use 0 if you make payments at the end of the period. If you leave out this argument, Excel assumes 0 (payments at the end of the period), which is usually what you want.

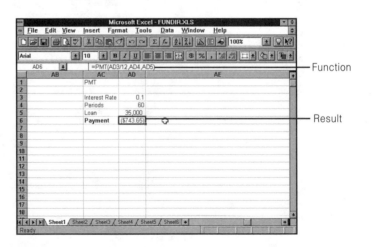

PPMT

=PPMT(rate,per,nper,pv,fv,type)

Calculates the principal paid during a single period of a loan.

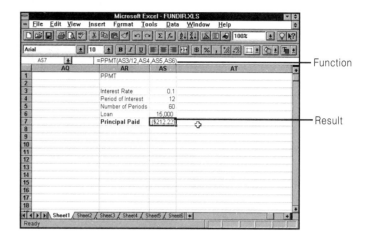

Function

Result

PV

=PV(rate,nper,pmt,fv,type)

Starts with the amount of money you can afford to pay monthly and then figures backward to tell you how much you can afford to borrow.

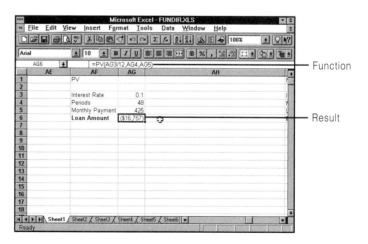

Function

Result

RATE

=RATE(nper,pmt,pv,fv,type,guess)

Calculates the rate you are paying on a loan. Note that you must enter the payment as a negative number (cash going out), and the result is the monthly interest rate. Multiply by 12 to get the annual rate.

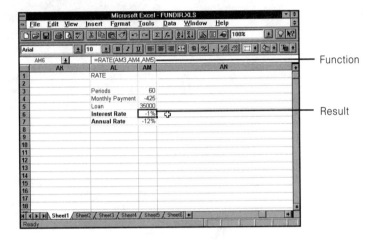

ROUND

=ROUND(number,num_digits)

Rounds a number to the number of digits that you specify.

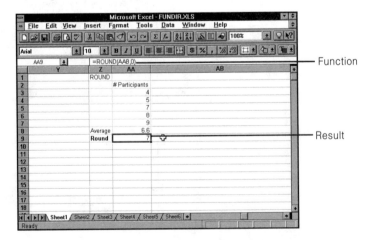

SUM

=SUM(number 1,number 2...)

Sums the numbers in parentheses. The numbers can be specific values, cells, or a range.

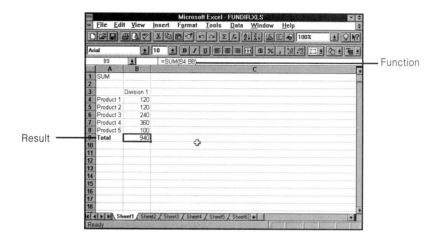

Index

Who cares what you think? WE DO!

We take our customers' opinions very personally. After all, you're the reason we publish these books. If you're not happy, we're doing something wrong.

We'd appreciate it if you would take the time to drop us a note or fax us a fax. A real person—not a computer—reads every letter we get, and makes sure that your comments get relayed to the appropriate people.

Not sure what to say? Here are some details we'd like to know:

- Who you are (age, occupation, hobbies, etc.)
- Where you bought the book
- Why you picked this book instead of a different one
- What you liked best about the book
- What could have been done better
- Your overall opinion of the book
- What other topics you would purchase a book on

Mail, e-mail, or fax it to:

Faithe Wempen
Product Development Manager

Alpha Books
201 West 103rd Street
Indianapolis, IN 46290

FAX: (317) 581-4669
CIS: 75430,174

Special Offer!

Alpha Books needs people like you to give opinions about new and existing books. Product testers receive free books in exchange for providing their opinions about them. If you would like to be a product tester, please mention it in your letter, and make sure you include your full name, address, and daytime phone.

Common Tasks

Starting Excel

1. Double-click on the Microsoft Office program group icon.

2. Double-click on the Microsoft Excel program icon.

Exiting Excel

1. Click on File in the menu bar.

2. Click on Exit.

Selecting a Menu Command

1. Click on the name of the menu you want to open.

2. Click on the command you want to execute.

3. If a dialog box appears, make the appropriate selections.

Using Dialog Boxes

To select	Do this
Tab	Click on the tab name to display the options for that tab.
Text box	Click in the text box, delete the current entry if necessary, and then type the new entry.
Spin box	Type an entry or click the spin arrows to scroll through the values.
List box	Click on the item you want in the list.
Drop-down list box	Click on the down arrow next to the item to display other selections. Then click on the item you want.
Check box	Click in the check box to turn on (check) or turn off (uncheck) the option.
Option button	Click in the option button to turn the option on (darkened) or off (blank).
Command button	Click the OK command button to confirm and carry out the command. Click the Cancel button to cancel the command.

Undoing a Command

- Select Edit Undo.

  OR

- Click the Undo button ↶.

Selecting a Range

1. Point to the first cell you want to select.

2. Hold down the left mouse button and drag across the other cells you want to select.

Selection Shortcuts

To select...	Do this...
An entire row	Click on the row number.
An entire column	Click on the column letter.
The entire worksheet	Click on the small box above the row numbers and to the left of the column letters.

Copying or Moving Cells

1. Select the range you want to move or copy.
2. To move the range, select the Edit Cut command or click on the Cut button ✂.

   OR

   Select the Edit Copy command or click on the Copy button 🖹 to copy the range.
3. Select the cell where you want to paste the range.
4. Select the Edit Paste command or click the Paste button 📋.

Saving a Document

1. Select the File Save command or click the Save button 💾.
2. Type a file name.
3. Click OK.

Closing a Document

- Select the File Close command.

  OR
- Double-click the Control-menu box.

Opening a Document

1. Select the File Open command or click the Open button 📂.
2. In the Open dialog box, type or click on the name of the file you want to open.
3. Click OK.

Previewing a Document

- Select the File Print Preview command.

  OR
- Click the Print Preview button 🔍.

Printing a Document

1. Select the File Print command or click the Print button 🖨.
2. Click OK.

Standard Toolbar

Button	Name	Description
	New Workbook	Creates a new workbook.
	Open	Displays the Open dialog box so that you can open a previously saved file.
	Save	Saves the workbook.
	Print	Prints the workbook currently on-screen.
	Print Preview	Changes to print preview.
	Spelling	Starts the spell checker.
	Cut	Cuts selected range to Clipboard.
	Copy	Copies selected range to Clipboard.
	Paste	Pastes data from Clipboard.
	Format Painter	Copies formatting.
	Undo	Undoes last command.
	Repeat	Repeats last command.
	AutoSum	Creates a sum function.
	Function Wizard	Starts the Function Wizard.
	Sort Ascending	Sorts selection in ascending order.
	Sort Descending	Sorts selection in descending order.
	Chart Wizard	Starts the Chart Wizard.
	Text Box	Creates a text box.
	Drawing	Displays the Drawing toolbar.
100%	Zoom Control	Enables you to zoom the worksheet to the percentage you specify.
	Tip Wizard	Starts the Tip Wizard.
	Help	Enables you to get context-sensitive help.

Formatting Toolbar

Button	Name	Description
Arial	Font	Enables you to select a font from a drop-down list.
10	Font Size	Enables you to select a font size from a drop-down list.
B	Bold	Applies bold to selected range.
I	Italic	Applies italic to selected range.
U	Underline	Underlines selected range.
Align Left	Align Left	Aligns selected range to the left.
Center	Center	Centers selected range.
Align Right	Align Right	Aligns selected range to the right
Center Across Columns	Center Across Columns	Centers text across selected range.
$	Currency Style	Applies currency style to the selected range.
%	Percent Style	Applies percent style to the selected range.
,	Comma Style	Applies comma style to the selected range.
Increase Decimal	Increase Decimal	Increases the number of decimal points displayed in the selected range.
Decrease Decimal	Decrease Decimal	Decreases the number of decimal points displayed in the selected range.
Borders	Borders	Enables you to select and apply borders to selected range.
Color	Color	Enables you to select and apply color to selected range.
Font Color	Font Color	Enables you to select and apply color to text in selected range.

Find the Features Most Useful to Use

Excel includes many, many features. Which features should you take time to learn? Which features will save you time? To find out, read the following table and check any statements that describe you. Then refer to the feature and page number to find help on that feature.

If you do this...	Investigate this feature
Perform complex calculations such as figuring loan payments or interest rate amounts	Functions, Chapter 13 and Appendix B
Want to use the same formula in other cells in the worksheet	Copy or Fill, Chapters 17 and 18
Want to fill a range with a series of numbers or dates	Fill, Chapter 18
Store sets of worksheets—for instance, one for each division	Worksheets, Chapter 19
Change how numbers appear	Number Format, Chapter 24
Make a column wider	Column Width, Chapter 25
Call attention to data on the worksheet	Borders, Patterns or Colors, Chapter 27 Drawing Tools, Chapter 42
Protect your worksheet from change	Protect Worksheet, Chapter 28
Use the same set of formatting (font, alignment, and so on)	Styles or Format Painter, Chapter 29
Set up your worksheet in a table format and don't want to mess with formatting	AutoFormat, Chapter 30
Have a two-page worksheet and want to print the row or column headings on the second page	Page Setup, Chapter 31
Don't want to print gridlines	Sheet Setup, Chapter 31
Shrink a worksheet so that it fits on one page	Sheet Setup, Chapter 31
Print a worksheet title, date, or other information on each page	Headers and Footers, Chapter 32
Forget a column or row	Insert, Chapter 35
Want to find an entry in the worksheet	Find, Chapter 37
Want to replace data in the worksheet	Replace, Chapter 37
Insert the same list of items in many worksheets	Custom Lists, Chapter 38

If you do this...	Investigate this feature
Want an easier way to refer to ranges	Range Names, Chapter 39
Make spelling mistakes	Spelling, Chapter 40
Can't find files you saved	Find File, Chapter 41
Keep track of lists of data	Database, Chapters 47 and 48
Want to create a logo or other simple drawing	Drawing Tools, Chapter 42
Want to show a visual representation of your data	Charts, Chapters 45 and 46

Function Reference

=AVERAGE(number 1,*number 2...***)**   Averages the numbers in parentheses.

=COUNT(value 1,*value 2...***)**   Counts the values in parentheses.

=FV(rate,nper,pmt,pv,*type***)**   Calculates the future value of an investment.

=IPMT(rate,per,nper,pv,*fv,type***)**   Calculates the interest paid during a single period of a loan.

=MAX(value 1,*value 2...***)**   Returns the largest value in a range.

=MIN(value 1,*value 2...***)**   Returns the lowest value in a range.

=NA()   Enters #NA in a cell so that it is clear which cells should contain values, but do not at this point.

=NOW()   Enters the current date and time in the worksheet cell.

=NPER(rate,pmt,pv,*fv,type***)**   Tells you how many payments you need to make on a loan.

=PMT(rate,nper,pv,*fv,type***)**   Figures the payment on a loan.

=PPMT(rate,per,nper,pv,*fv,type***)**   Calculates the principal paid during a single period of a loan.

=PV(rate,nper,pmt,fv,*type***)**   Starts with the amount of money you can afford to pay monthly and then figures backward to tell you how much you can afford to borrow.

=RATE(nper,pmt,pv,*fv,type,guess***)**   Calculates the rate you are paying on a loan. Note that you must enter the payment as a negative number (cash going out).

=ROUND(number,num_digits)   Rounds a number to the number of digits that you specify.

=SUM(number 1,*number 2...***)**   Sums the numbers in parentheses. The numbers can be specific values, cells, or a range.